HOW TO WIN IN THE GOVERNMENT MARKET

Hundreds of useful tips
from two of the
most experienced
GovCon experts

by

Mark Amtower
&
Michael Lisagor

How to Win in the Government Market

Published by Government Market Press
on the Amazon KDP publishing platform

Copyright 2022 Mark Amtower & Michael Lisagor

Printed in the United States of America

10 9 8 7 6 5 4 3 2 1

Library of Congress Cataloging-in-Publication Data

ISBN: 9798786985147

Nonfiction > Business & Economics > Marketing
Nonfiction > Business & Economics > Sales & Selling

TABLE OF CONTENTS

Foreword by Nick Wakeman	5
About the Authors	7
Relationships are the key to GovCon Success	9
Plan for company growth	12
Seven GovCon myths that need busting	18
Sell is not always a four-letter word	22
The Prospect Marketing Pyramid	23
Why small businesses don't graduate	27
What's Account Based Marketing?	28
Lowest price technically acceptable sucks	31
Agency based marketing drives results	34
Performance in a virtual workplace	37
Understand your market channels	40
Essential capture plan components	43
How GovCon executives should use LinkedIn	57
Seize the future with we-government	59
Numbers don't lie: Feds are on LinkedIn	61
Stay in your target market	64
Social selling fiscal end - COVID & beyond	66
Make your marketing dollars count	69
Does traditional PR still matter?	72
Line staff need to talk about growth	74
The act of being on LinkedIn is marketing	76
Turn budget fear into opportunity	79
Habits of successful LinkedIn networkers	81
Just say no to bad bids	85
LinkedIn's fiscal year end power	87
When to ask for the sale	89
Small businesses need to stand out	94
Five habits of incompetent BD executives	97
Questions to ask when seeking outside help	99
How to assess a company's sales health	102

SOCIAL SELLING CHANGES YOUR BID DECISIONS	104
BASIC LABOR RATE TERMINOLOGY	107
HOW TO CRACK THE WT TOP 100	110
SO, YOU'RE A NEW MANAGER	113
DON'T MAKE THESE THREE LINKEDIN MISTAKES	116
BREAKING UP IS HARD TO DO	119
AMTOWER'S RULES OF SPEAKER ENGAGEMENT	121
WHAT TO ASK SALES JOB CANDIDATES	124
SMALL BUSINESS CONTRACTORS' NEW YEAR TO-DO'S	125
THE POWER OF OLD-FASHIONED CONVERSATIONS	127
WHY DON'T SOME SMALL BUSINESSES WIN MORE?	130
FIND THE RIGHT LEAD TRACKING SYSTEM	133
LEVERAGING MARKETING RESOURCES IS CRITICAL	136
HOW TO ASSESS CUSTOMER INFLUENCE	139
DON'T BE A WALDO – STAND OUT	141
MUST-HAVE BID PURSUIT AND DECISION PROCESSES	144
FIVE STEPS TO STAND OUT FROM THE CROWD	150
CRITICAL ELEMENTS OF A WINNING PROPOSAL	153
FIVE CONSIDERATIONS TO START THE NEW YEAR	166
KNOW ALL YOUR CONTRACT REQUIREMENTS	169
THREE FISCAL YEAR END TACTICS	171
MANAGE CLIENT EXPECTATIONS	174
SHORT ATTENTION SPANS ARE A CHALLENGE	176
START RE-COMPETE PREPARATION EARLY	180
SIX TIPS FOR SURVIVING AS A CONSULTANT	184
AFTERWORD: WHY WE WROTE THIS BOOK	187

Foreword by Nick Wakeman
Editor-in-Chief, Washington Technology

You're holding a collection of advice and insights on the government market from a pair of old hands who have pretty much seen it all.

Mark Amtower and Mike Lisagor have advised thousands of executives and companies in the government market over the years with guidance on marketing, strategic planning, personnel, and, yes, even a little bit on self-promotion.

As you read these essays, you'll find Amtower and Lisagor return to several themes over and over – the importance of relationships and communications; the power of strategic planning; and the criticality of understanding your market and your customers.

It also is obvious that they love the government market, but they don't shy away from offering some tough love. They aren't afraid to talk about common mistakes and tweak a few egos along the way.

One of my favorites is the essay, Five Habits of Incompetent BD Executives. You'll cringe a little when you read that one because we all know someone guilty of at least two of those bad habits.

The advice you'll find in this collection ranges from broad, almost philosophical discussions such as the essays The Power of the Old-Fashioned Conversation and Seize the Future with

We-Government, to very action-oriented advice such as the essay Social Selling Changes Your Bid Decisions and several essays that discuss how to use LinkedIn.

Something else that is very apparent is that Amtower and Lisagor want you to succeed and what they offer here is a treasure chest of information and insights. Each essay is a nugget that you can use as you drive your organization forward.

And some are fodder for those in the mirror conversations that we have with ourselves when we've either suffered a defeat or we're about to step forward into something new and bold.

I think more than anything, Amtower and Lisagor want you to be smart about the market, understand the common pitfalls and mistakes, and to be unafraid.

Let their essays be your guide to finding success in the GovCon market.

About the authors

Consultant, speaker, author, and radio host Mark Amtower is one of the most recognized professionals in the government market. Amtower is widely known for his candor in his articles, consulting, radio interviews, presentations, and keynotes. He is also known for all black attire and not wearing ties. His consultancy, Amtower & Company, was founded in 1985. He has been quoted in over 200 publications worldwide and has been interviewed on over 75 radio shows, webinars and podcasts in the US, Canada, and the UK. Amtower's weekly radio show, Amtower Off Center, airs Monday at noon on Federal News Network (www.FederalNewsNetwork.com).

Mark's first book, *Government Marketing Best Practices* (2005), was the best-selling GovCon book published between 2001-2009, selling 9,000 copies. He next wrote, *Why Epiphanines Never Occur to Couch Potatoes* (2007), and then *Selling to the Government* (Wiley, 2010) -- one of the most comprehensive books available on doing business with the government. Mark lives with wife in Maryland. He can be reached on LinkedIn.

Starting in the 1970s, Michael Lisagor worked as a government contractor hardware and software engineer, IT project manager, business developer, and a domestic and international vice president.

In 1999, he relinquished his suit and tie to start a consulting company, Celerity Works, where he advised over 60 contractors on how to win more government business. A FED100 awardee, he has written numerous articles for

Washington Technology and Federal Computer, was the co-founder of the annual Federal Program Management Summit, implemented the acquisition risk management process at GSA FEDSIM, and is one of the co-founders of GovFlex.com where he developed the Government Contractor Knowledge Academy. He was also an adjunct marketing professor at National Louis University.

Lisagor has written four books related to doing business with the government: *How to Develop a Winning Small Business Innovation Research (SBIR) Proposal (w/Eric Adolphe)*, *Winning and Managing Government Business*, *The Enlightened Manager*, and *The Essential Guide to Managing a Government Project (*published in 2021).

Mike is also the author of *Romancing the Buddha 3rd edition*, *Personal Growth in the Time of COVID*, and *My Fifty Years of Buddhist Practice*. Mike now spends most of his time writing articles and books plus playing harmonica and singing in a local blues band. He lives with his wife of 50+ years on an island in the Pacific Northwest. Mike can be reached on LinkedIn and mike@celerityworks.com.

Relationships are the key to GovCon Success

This 2018 Washington Technology year-end wrap up column was not so much to inform others but to remind myself why relationships are the key to marketing success…a common theme in both Mike and my chapters in this book. - Mark

I've had discussions lately with several of my well-known government contracting friends, collaborators, and advisors on what drives this market. The consensus was the Big R: *relationships.*

It's impossible to overstate the role of relationships in GovCon (Government Contracting). They are needed to engage with customers, prospects, primes and subs, and OEMs via channel, social and print media, and internal relationships within your company. I thought I'd share several examples of ways I've re-engaged with my rather large GovCon network in the hope some will resonate with you.

In 37 years, I've only joined a few organizations in our market, primarily because I believe if you join you need to actively engage. I'm a busy guy, so finding or making time to participate wasn't always a priority which was a mistake on my part.

So, I've recently joined AFCEA and am now on their Small Business Committee where I've met several interesting people and have renewed acquaintances with former colleagues. I also spoke at the Professional Services Council's new Marketing and Communications Network, and they've invited me to attend some subsequent meetings.

Picking the right association venue(s) for you and your company is critical to your professional survival and growth.

Once again, I had an active speaking calendar this year with Government Marketing University's GAIN conference, the Government IT Sales Summit, Government Blockchain Association, the Tower Club GovCon group, 930Gov, APMP, and several others. I get to network at each, seeing old friends and meeting new people. I attend briefings hosted by *Washington Technology*, Bloomberg Government, and GovExec for both information and networking.

Events, including seminars, conferences, briefings, are a cornerstone of relationship building.

I started using the Calendly application (https://calendly.com/markamtower) so people could reserve time for a short call. The app shows up in my email signature line. I also started working LinkedIn harder to stay on the radar among my first-degree connections – and it's working.

You know the annoying email that reminds you of birthdays, new positions and more? I'm now responding to each one of those that comes through, and the results are palpable.

Most people respond to say thanks for acknowledging my birthday, new job, etc. But with some it sets off a whole new conversation, something along the lines of "I've been meaning to call/get in touch about…" I look at their profiles before sending a congratulations note and am often reminded that they are involved in something one of my clients should know about, so I do a message with a note to explain why we need to connect.

These are the low-hanging fruit of social selling, and they help you nurture the relationships you've built into a vibrant network.

Over the period of just one week, I had interesting exchanges with, among others, Bruce Tucker (Planet Technologies), my favorite Admin Assistant Sheila Deane (GDIT), Lynn Welch (Education Management Solutions), Sheryle Thompson (Allied Telesis), my new friend Amber Hart (The Pulse of Government Contracting), and Brian Green (Learning Tree International).

Will all these generate new business? Of course not. But each will keep me closer in the top of their mind and some will come to fruition.

Why? Because now we know each other.

Should this matter to you? Only if you want fruitful relationships in our market. It's truly not optional!

Plan for company growth

I first recognized the need for a more streamlined strategic planning approach in the early 90s. I then codified it into a practice model with Bill Hoover, currently the chairman of American Systems ~2001. - Mike

"Thinking is the hardest work there is, which is probably the reason so few engage in it." - Henry Ford

Managers often complain about conflicting and changing priorities, vague targets, unpredictable results, unsound investment strategies, unclear lines of authority and responsibility, management confusion and staff frustration. Too many government contractor executives echo Lily Tomlin's lament: *"I always wanted to be somebody, but I should have been more specific."*

There are many articles and books about how to write a business plan. But the real challenge — what separates the slow-growth organizations from the barnstormers — is a leader's willingness to develop a business strategy that consists of clear and measurable objectives and has the support of key staff and is used throughout the year to measure progress and make decisions. Here's an example:

- Increase financial value
- Grow market share in target markets
- Improve customer satisfaction
- Increase employee satisfaction
- Gain recognition for core technologies

The age of omnipotent business leaders is over. And although this top-down only management model may produce near-term results, eventually even the most loyal subjects will rebel. Too many managers still haven't learned that input from employees is crucial to successfully identifying the internal factors that will affect the organization's ability to sustain reasonable growth. And external changes in enabling technologies, budget and policy, market/citizen demand, competitor strategies and resource supply also need to be reflected in the business plan.

Paula, a Washington, D.C. native, had a CEO who recently took a vacation to Taiwan and came back determined to do business there. Unfortunately, her company barely had the back-office staff to do the payroll and contracts much less deal with all the aspects of international contracting. The company lost a few hundred thousand dollars chasing this business and the negative impact on domestic business growth was measurable.

I don't have enough fingers to count the times I've seen this happen in small businesses. It is evidence of the absence of and inability to adhere to a practical business planning process.

The figure on the next page illustrates the relationship between a company's mission (your purpose for being in business), vision (what the company will look like in five years), strategic envelope (the services/products and target agencies you will concentrate on), breakthrough objectives (the objectives, if achieved, that will have the most impact on growth), and priority actions (the most important steps to take to achieve the objectives). This process should then drive business development and marketing plans. Companies should also obtain a thorough knowledge of the government marketplace. This information is readily available on the web and from market research companies and consultants. It should include overall Federal, state, and local government and individual agency budgets, priorities, and key technologies as well as major program initiatives, incumbent contractors and buying practices. This will allow the companies to better match its products and services with specific agency needs because what you're selling isn't as important if they don't want to buy it.

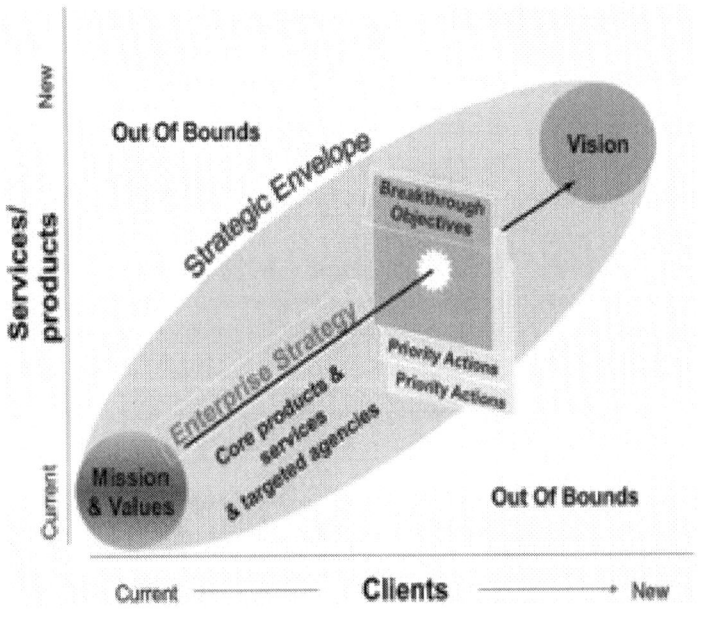

It is also important for companies to carefully consider their value proposition. There are at least three types or levels of professional services companies or services divisions of product companies in the government marketplace:

1. High-end professional services. These have high wrap rates (and labor rates) that reflect their bonus structure, large training budget, internal R&D, and product development overhead, and, frankly, company cache!

2. Mid-level services contractors/integrators. These have competitive wrap rates but not rock bottom. The range varies depending on the competition, the agency and company cost center that is bidding the job. Many of these larger companies have separate lower cost business units to compete on services jobs like range support contracts (# 3 below).

3. Low-end/highly competitive services contractors (includes many small and mid-size companies). These companies usually have pockets of very qualified technical staff and PMs and then a whole bunch of mid to junior level technical folks. They compete on GSA schedules and government wide acquisition contracts and offer average benefits to their employees. They also don't typically support product development overhead in their labor cost pools.

Government sales staff almost always must balance between "give me more competitive rates" and "give me higher technical quality/solutions." This is a healthy push/pull that goes on in growing companies. It influences how you approach the market and your sales pitch.

Business leaders who run their own strategic planning meetings aren't always open to suggestions from staff about different strategies. How willing are employees to express their true opinions, especially in an open forum? A strong outside facilitator can usually level the playing field enough to allow an honest exchange of ideas, but even the world's most enlightened facilitator won't succeed if the leader resists change.

Incentive plans should reward behaviors and results that are consistent with strategic objectives. But strategic plans alone don't guarantee business growth — action plans do.

Strategic objectives must be translated into relevant and measurable actions assigned to individuals who are held accountable. Similarly, strategic actions should be monitored. If you don't care enough to ask your staff for a status report, they won't care enough to perform.

Finally, prioritize and estimate the cost and return on investment of each action. Then match all the actions with the operating budget. Only implement what's affordable. I've worked with several organizations that have developed a gigantic list of actions, only to turn them over to managers for implementation in their spare time. This almost never works.

Also, if I hear one more business manager declare, *"We need to get it done with sweat equity,"* I'm going to scream! Aligning your investments with what you're talking about takes courage. But it's the only reliable way to become a successful company.

But how do you uncover what needs fixing? We've all heard the story about the emperor who had no clothes. Unfortunately, this phenomenon exists in too many government contractors. A leader's unwillingness to periodically self-assess and his/her staff's unwillingness to provide honest feedback can be a tremendous growth inhibitor.

To identify the specific business areas in need of improvement, have an independent expert perform a business growth assessment. This type of analysis can be conducted as a combination of a web survey and key staff interviews. Everything from the effectiveness of strategic planning to sales and proposal management should be considered. Capabilities that should be evaluated include:

- Strategic planning process and adherence
- Core services/solutions and target agency alignment and focus
- Marketing strategy and execution
- Business development staff performance
- Opportunity qualification and capture management (new and re-compete)
- Pursuit and bid decision process
- Proposal development and review process

This type of periodic assessment is crucial to business success. Identified gaps in the business growth process can be translated into breakthrough objectives and priority actions with a reasonable assurance that precious resources are applied to the improvements that will make the most difference. Successful contractors often employ this type of process. And it is the only way I know to overcome institutionalized crisis management and a low win rate.

Seven GovCon myths that need busting

Both Mike and I have collected numerous myths about doing business with the government. Here's my take! – Mark

Depending on where you start on the journey of doing business with the government, you'll hear things that may not necessarily be accurate, and in some cases, intentionally inaccurate. Right away, when you register at SAM.gov, you'll get phone calls from some questionable people offering the magic elixir, telling you they can get you a GSA Schedule and it will bring in tons of money, real soon. This is just the beginning.

I get contacted frequently from the quarrelsome and contentious newbies (see John Locke, Second Treatise on Civil Government, chapter 5) complaining about not getting government work after visiting an agency Office of Small, Disadvantaged Business Utilization, getting a GSA Schedule, or perhaps burning incense. "But I was told…" is the way the conversation usually starts. And it often ends with, "it's just not fair."

"Fair" is an illusion and there is no "level playing field." So, let's dispel some of these myths in the hope that some will read this chapter before they enter the market.

Myth Seven: 8(a), service-disabled, veteran-owned small business, woman-owned small business, or some other set-aside status guarantees government contracts.

Let's be clear, there are no guarantees for anyone in this market. A set-aside status may help get access to bidding on some work or joining an industry team, but it doesn't guarantee a win.

Myth Six: Winning a spot on an IDIQ or getting a GSA Schedule guarantees business.

Winning a spot on an IDIQ is not easy, so most companies do end up making money, to greater or lesser degrees. But there have been some instances where a prime spot got the company zip, nada, zilch. On the GSA Schedule, making no money happens frequently. I started tracking GSA sales in the mid-1990s and the bottom third of the contractors made little or nothing. They just didn't know how to sell from a Schedule.

Myth Five: End of fiscal spending, aka, "the feeding frenzy" or the "budget flush" is the best time to clean up.

During the era of the perpetual continuing resolution, end of fiscal year spending has always been difficult for feds. Often, they really don't know how much money they'll have come September. The experienced contractor knows to queue up potential business early, aligning the need, the funding, and the contractual vehicle with the client agency well in advance of September. If there are pockets of money left (and there will be), the agency will have pre-selected and prioritized places to spend it. The less fortunate contractor will be buying advertisements that will likely not pay dividends.

Myth Four: Meeting the CIO at some photo-op event will lead to preferential treatment.

Among the calls I get are those asking which if they should attend a certain event, often preceded by, "The CIO of X agency will be there…" CIOs are too often in the job for as little as 18 months. Meet the program managers and the career senior executive service folks, people who will be there managing programs and projects long after the CIO vacates for the private sector. There are many important events. But attending just to meet a CIOs is often not the best use of your time. Are some CIOs exceptions? Certainly.

Myth Three: Five inexpensive people straight out of college pounding the phones is a better approach than hiring one of those expensive, lunch eating BD people who are never in the office.

Make no mistake, this is a relationship driven market, and good BD people know key players in the agencies they work. They know when there is money, they know the contractual vehicles in play, and they have a good idea about when the deal will come to fruition. If you're selling #2 Ticonderoga pencils, you may have success with the phone jockeys.

Myth Two: Sub-contracting is the easiest way to gain entry to the market.

I've heard that SBA representatives give a list of primes contractors to small businesses and say, "Call these people. They need subcontractors." A cold call to a prime or an unprepared visit to a small business liaison office is the first step to being ignored forever by that prime. They usually have a short list of key factors that subs must bring to the table, things like a truly unique skill set required by the contract, relationships inside the client organization, and a working knowledge of problems that agency is dealing with. Your set-aside status is not at the top of the list.

Myth One: Entering the government market is fast, easy, lucrative, and painless.

When you register at SAM.gov your phone will ring. On the other end of the line, you will hear a variation of this theme: "We can help you hit the ground running by getting you a GSA Schedule, winning you set-aside business, getting you on the "short list" of insiders and more. When you hear these carefully crafted, hyperbolic assertions, hang up.

There is no magic formula and there are no short cuts for getting into this business. The only short cut is learning the market inside out, then focusing on your niche.

But make no mistake, it's a long-term game.

Sell is not always a four-letter word

I've talked about this topic over 100 times including at one restaurant where the power shut off and I had to talk in the dark! – Mike

Unfortunately, there are a lot of reasons managers – most people for that matter – respond negatively to the word **sell**. Depending on their experience with salespeople, this can range from a mild aversion to outright repulsion. (Note: Don't hire this person to do your federal sales!)

It's not the word that is the problem but rather how "sell" or sales is done and the motive behind it.

As a former program manager and then business developer, I always tried to view sales as an opportunity to make friends. People react much more positively when approached by someone who's genuinely interested in understanding what they do every day and what keeps them up at night. This is as opposed to being confronted by someone whose only interest is pushing their product or service. Company managers need to understand this difference and try to overcome their reluctance to talk to their federal clients about their new requirements.

I have a longtime friend who claims I'm the world's best salesperson because I have sold my wife an inferior product for over 50 years! And, while that was the case when we first met in high school, my service offering has greatly improved as I've learned to really listen, understand her needs, and respect her boundaries, not just my own.

The Prospect Marketing Pyramid

Here's my "rebranded" marketing pyramid from a December 2021 LinkedIn article. - Mark

In the early 1990s I expanded my consulting to go after B2B catalogers and introduce them to the then lucrative world of B2G. These were still the early days of the government charge card (then IMPAC card, now SmartPay) and for established brand catalogers, this was a ripe new territory where there were still nice margins.

I got to work with some great companies and even hosted my own B2G Catalog Summit for six years, from the late-1990s until the early 2000s.

I also spoke at several B2B (business to business) events, met several well-known experts in B2B, and stumbled across a concept called the ***"prospect pyramid."***

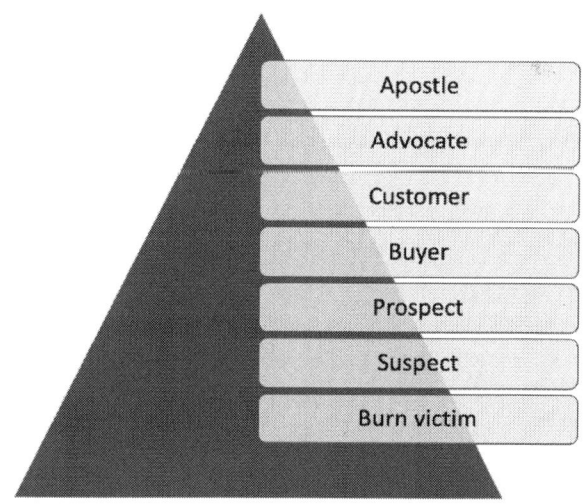

The idea was simple: those who could possibly buy your product were *"suspects"* (bottom of the pyramid), but they probably didn't know you.

The next level up was *"prospects"*, those who knew you but were not yet buying from you.

After that was *"buyer"*, probably a one-off buyer who may or may not return.

Then there were *"customers"*, those who bought from you on a regular basis.

One variation of the pyramid had another level, *"advocates,"* customers who bought regularly and talked about you favorably.

Around the time I discovered the pyramid I had a very bad in-store experience with Best Buy, and I have not set foot in a Best Buy for well over 20 years. I still tell the story at some conferences.

So, it occurred to me that there was at least one other level at the bottom of the pyramid- the *"burn victim"* – someone who disliked your company so much that when anyone mentioned it, they become apoplectic. We all have those stories. My latest burn victim story is Nike, where customer service doesn't exist…don't get me started.

There were companies on the other end of the spectrum as well, companies that I love to buy from as their products are good and the service is above and beyond.

Nordstrom was mine at that time. I was switching from conventional business attire (I wore three-piece suits with matching braces and ties) to the all-black, no tie look that has become part of my brand in GovCon. Most of you don't remember me in non-black. Anyway, I had this guy in Nordstrom who'd call me when anything in my size (I'm not an easy fit) came in. And I would only buy from him.

I became a Nordstrom *apostle,* and I gave others the business card of *my* Nordstrom guy. So, at the top of my pyramid, we have apostles, those who love your company and proselytize on your behalf frequently.

The pyramid became part of my half-day workshop, Government Marketing Best Practices, which became a book in 2005. The prospect pyramid description is on pages 39-44 if you happen to have a copy of *Government Marketing Best Practices.*

The entire customer experience (CX) movement has been revitalized recently, but it has been with us for quite some time. The work of JoAnna Brandi, Jeanne Bliss, and more recently Martha Dorris all emphasize the importance of the customer experience. Vic Hunter's 1997 gem, *Business to Business Marketing- Creating a Community of Customers,* had a huge influence on my thinking.

But like I write in *Best Practices,* your pyramid shouldn't simply focus on those who buy from you, but also others in your sphere of influence: media, vendor partners, employees and former employees, investors, anyone with whom you interact.

Your conduct, how you treat all of those around you, impacts you directly or indirectly, now and in the future.

For each of us, everyone we interact with falls somewhere on our own prospect pyramid, the one people measure you by. When your name comes up, what do people think or say?

I wish I could say that I've always treated everyone well so that they would at least be near the top of my pyramid, but sadly that is not the case.

Why small businesses don't graduate

I wrote this for a presentation I did in 2007. The slides wouldn't fit in our book!

There are numerous reasons so many small businesses in the 8(a), HUB zone, SDVOB, WOSB, and similar programs fail to successfully graduate to the full and open procurement environment. Put another way, there are several steps small businesses should take to become to a larger competitive company. In my earlier career, I experienced two effective graduations and, since then, several others with consulting clients. Among the challenges were:

- An inadequate strategic planning process
- The absence of a mature business development, capture and proposal process and resources
- A lack of well-defined core competencies or technical discriminators
- Poorly defined value propositions
- Insufficient support organization infrastructure
- Not enough experience bidding on full and open bids
- Over reliance on just a few agencies
- Too few strategic partnerships including with new emerging small businesses able to compete on future set-asides and re-competes
- Unwillingness or inability of the founder(s) to either become a more effective leader and/or to delegate responsibility and authority

Why not avoid making the same mistakes over again?

What's Account Based Marketing?

I've been writing about Account Based Marketing and why my clients should start small before going wide for decades. – Mark

Among the hotter topics in the business-to-business market is the notion of account-based marketing or ABM. Translated into Gov-speak, this is agency-based marketing, which many have been doing for years

However, seeing as it's hot in B2B, I thought I'd share a simple ABM formula I've used with companies for the past 25-plus years. It's a five-step approach and it works. Here is the short version.

Step 1: Pick the target agency(cies). Where do you have a beachhead in an agency? Are you known by agency influencers? Is your agency presence exploitable? Exploitable simply means is there a real opportunity for you to grow.

Do agency requirements correlate to the services and products your company provides?

Are you on the contractual vehicles the agency prefers? If not, can you get a slot as a sub-contractor. Can you team as a subcontractor or bid as a prime on an upcoming procurement?

I recall what Bob Davis, an incumbent who has been at specific agencies forever, told me: "Market share is rented, never owned."

Step 2: Map the influencers. If you know who some of the main players are, map them out on LinkedIn. From here, flesh out the likely organizational chart and develop a connection strategy. Don't simply reach out with a generic "I'd like you to join my network."

Are any of them attending any industry functions? Look for their names as speakers or panelists at industry events and plan on being there. Attend events focused on that agency, including the seemingly mundane Office of Small business Utilization events.

LinkedIn always plays a major role in mapping and connecting. After all, this is a relationship driven market.

See Mike's chapter on how to identify agency influencers.

Step 3: Do the research. There are multiple sources of information such as the Federal Procurement Data System, the agency web site, OMB 53 and 300 filings, agency news on trade media websites.
If you subscribe to Bloomberg or Deltek, get an agency specific report.

Identify any agency-specific contracts you should be on. Are they coming up for re-compete? Who are the major competitors?

When I'm working with a company, I create Google Alerts for all pertinent information. This provides me way too much information, but as I wade through it, I always find useful nuggets.

Step 4: Develop a content calendar and content delivery strategy. Good content (e.g., social media and blog posts,

LinkedIn articles, white papers) will help you build credibility with your audience. It allows you to share your knowledge of the agency and the problems it faces. It allows you to offer viable solutions to those problems. The content is the result of your conversations with influencers and your research.

Your subject matter experts should be at the forefront of your content strategy, as they need to be positioned as the key players the agency needs to move forward.

Your content calendar will ensure a regular stream of information for your targeted agency. A one-off white paper buried on your web site is not a content strategy.

There are multiple venues for sharing content. Depending on your budget, you may work with a media outlet and/or you may deploy through various social platforms.

See my later chapters for more on content marketing.

Step 5: Expand the beachhead. Make sure your front line, sales and business development staff are knowledgeable about key agency connections and fully armed with relevant research and content.

Marketing should be getting constant feedback from outside staff to adjust the content and validate the current research. Donuts and coffee once a month are a great way to get feedback, as are one-on-one meetings with top performers.

This is not a linear program, it's a circular program, where Step 5 always leads back to Step 1.

ABM may still be getting traction in B2B, but for B2G it needs to be part of our genetic code.

Lowest price technically acceptable sucks

I wrote this for Federal Computer Week in response to a survey I conducted that showed that most of the government and industry managers were opposed to the practice of awarding contracts to contractors that were, "barely technically acceptable!" But, alas, some things never change. – Mike

In the late 1980s, when my daughters were in elementary school and my grandkids were only a possibility, I worked at a large government services provider. Like many other contractors, we were forced to create separate organizations and cost centers to compete for an increasing number of Lowest Price Technically Acceptable (LPTA) contracts. It started with less skilled tasks but eventually expanded to encompass even high-end consulting and technical support contracts. Naïve me - I thought we buried this practice with procurement reform in the nineties.

Now comes the news that a major contractor is restructuring -- perhaps in response to this same phenomenon. I'm also seeing a disturbing trend of incumbent contractors losing re-competes to lower priced competitors who are bidding as much as 40% to 60% reduced fully burdened labor rates and less than enough staff to perform the work. Is anyone still doing cost realism assessments? And who's making these awards and why?

Here are five possible explanations and reasons why government executives should discourage this practice before it becomes a tidal wave:

Number Five: Would you interview and then hire the job candidate who just barely meets your minimum requirements? Well, that is what you're doing when you establish LPTA evaluation criteria. Taxpayers deserve the best value for a reasonable amount of money. Not the least value for the least money.

Number Four: There is no such as thing as "non-mission critical services." Are you really willing to trust your productivity to a network maintained only by college graduates? Or your safety to a building designed by apprentice architects? Every agency's mission depends on these services.

Number Three: What's more important? Mission success or cost savings? How many of the major program failures and cost overruns of the 80's and 90's could have been prevented if contractors were allowed to provide the best available qualified staff?

Number Two: Buying a pencil? Get the lowest price. Buying program support or information technology solution design? Hire the best and brightest. Don't settle for less.

Number One: This one is for Congressional, OMB and agency executives. Even source selection officials don't have the necessary clout to overrule dictated overall budget reductions. Everyone is running scared. The required fiscal prioritization and cultural change must start at the top.

I think we all realize this is going to be an industry reality for quite some time. But let's not kid ourselves. The last time this happened there were serious repercussions. Higher attrition rates. Lower past performance. More business failures. Loss of corporate and agency knowledge and experience. So, share your concerns with government contracting officers and program managers. Let Congressional, Senate and OMB staffers understand the negative impacts of LPTA.

Let's make sure they all know that, to quote Yogi Berra, this is "*Déjà vu all over again.*"

Agency based marketing drives results

Here's an example of why and how one small business has thrived by making ABM part of their business development culture. – Mark

Probably 90 percent of the small companies that have contacted me over the years about entering the GovCon market start with the premise of selling to "the government" without bothering to figure out where their product or service fit best. From that it's not a stretch to say that they haven't thought of which agency, or agencies, would be the best target.

Even smalls that have been in the market for a couple years get the itch to go wide, to sell to more agencies. If you have the right government-wide contract vehicle and the right products or services, that might not be a bad strategy.

But for most small contractors, focusing on one or two agencies is often the best strategy, especially if you have already established a beachhead. This can be in the form of a sub-contract that has allowed you to build some relationships and establish a little past performance, or it can be smaller prime contracts.

Agency-based marketing (ABM) can be used for a specific campaign, like landing a spot on a contract, or it can be used as a growth strategy for the long-term.

Resource Management Concepts (RMC), a small contractor in Lexington Park, MD, is a great example. Lexington Park is home to the Patuxent River Naval Air Station, widely known as Pax River. Soon to celebrate its 30th anniversary, RMC has focused largely on Pax River and NAWCAD, Naval Air Warfare Center Aircraft Division, for the past three decades, growing from a very small business in 1992, to a large small business in 2021, with 460 employees and $75 million in revenue.

While RMC has some business in other agencies, it has largely focused its key skills areas, RDT&E and scientific computing, on NAWCAD. CEO Kevin Cooley told me "We've been especially successful at focusing on specific captures that can provide high revenue or new capabilities/past performance and capturing them with laser precision."

Almost four years ago, they started looking to other areas of the US Navy that also required RDT&E and scientific computing services. SPAWAR (now NIWC) came up as a likely target. NIWC has two major locations: San Diego (primary location) NIWC-PAC, and Charleston, NIWC-ATL.

RMC developed a plan to attack NIWC. They leased a Charleston office, hired a local BD professional, gained presence as a subcontractor, developed partner relationships, and got active in the Charleston Defense Contractors Association (CDCA).

When the NIWC LANT's RDT&E Network Services contract was announced, RMC had been on the ground in Charleston for over 3 years. They knew the key people needed to win the contract and went after it, landing the PM from an incumbent on a different NIWC research contract. She also happened to be on the Board of Advisors for CDCA. They had already established relationships and credibility with key IT NIWC personnel. By the time the NIWC contract was announced, RMC was an established provider for them in Charleston.

RMC is a poster child for how long-term ABM focus, dedication, building relationships with an agency and the local community pays great dividends.

Performance in a virtual workplace

I wrote this article about telework for Govloop in 2009. Perhaps a premonition of COVID isolation? – Mike

I'm wearing my grungy sweatpants and torn Oakland Raiders T-shirt as I write this column in my home office on an island in the Puget Sound. My editor in Falls Church, Va., rarely sees me, and I suspect would be somewhat appalled at my work attire. Fortunately, he values results over appearance and office visibility.

The rapid expansion of teleworking in the government workplace means that more civil servants are also spending their time at home. Like me, they sit in front of a monitor and use e-mail and wikis to communicate from a distance. Unlike me, they may not have such a tangible work product to demonstrate their time spent and prove their value to the organization.

So how do their managers see what these remote staff members are doing? How do they identify and reward the hard workers and get the slackers to either move up or move out? At a time when many managers hail from the aging baby-boomer generation but newer Gen X, Y, and Z workers are gadget-savvy, how do they connect in the cyber office?

One of my clients, Janice, a senior federal agency information technology manager, worried that she might be overlooking industrious staff members who quietly toiled behind the scenes in favor of those who were more able and/or adept at getting face time. Having more than half her staff spread through three different states was challenging her ability to accurately evaluate personnel performance.

For many years, she used the venerable "management by walking around" approach. Of course, that was only possible when all the employees worked in the same office. Now she was forced to put more emphasis on measured contribution than on physical observation.

Large commercial outfits are using workforce performance management software applications to monitor these individual and organizational objectives. They are even having serious business planning and status meetings via collaborative Web sites and fourth-dimensional worlds such as Second Life.

So, Janice established a few prioritized measures of success for each organizational unit and employee, and then regularly measured and communicated the results. The year-end business results and employee satisfaction survey showed significant improvement.

Veteran managers need to embrace these innovative technologies or face alienating an ever-increasing number of Web-savvy workers. This means a cultural transition from face-to-face encounters at the water cooler to webcams, blogs, and groupware.

What's more, midlevel and frontline managers don't need to wait for official direction from above to make some of these changes right away. While always considering security and privacy restrictions, they can use the positions and authority they do have to explore ways to integrate some of these solutions. Who knows? It could be a first step toward creating the organization they hope to inherit in the next 10 years.

As more telework employees and their managers are learning, office familiarity is not an acceptable substitute for real performance. Hopefully, our next generation of government leaders will find the patience to help us gray-haired — or in my case, no-haired — managers adapt to new ways.

Understand your market channels

Here are the highlights of a 2019 content marketing survey.
– Mark

Market Connections third content marketing study in 2019 was entitled Content Marketing Review: Federal & Beyond. This year the study includes state and local governments. I strongly suggest you download the slides from the briefing. After sharing the demographics, the study has sections on Most Valuable Content (segmented by products, services, and emerging tech), Important Content Features, Content Placement, Content Source, Time Spent (on content), Content Engagement, and Key Takeaways. There are separate statistics for federal and state and local and education in each section. The slides from the briefing provide a deep dive into the value of content in the government contracting market. I can only imagine the depth the full report offers.

Here are a few of the many takeaways:

- Fourteen types of content are included.
- Content without sales messages is preferred.
- For products, services and emerging tech, these formats make the top five: product demos, research reports, white papers, case studies.
- Webinars and Marketing Collateral each make it into the top five three times.
- The top three features of content are the same for Fed and SLED: Data and research to support content, product specs, and examples of past performance.

- Twelve online venues for both Fed and SLED were ranked for effectiveness, with these four being in the top five for each: search engines, corporate web sites, government focused online communities, and government news web sites.

In a way, there are no major surprises in the study, except perhaps the order that some things appear.

Moderator Aaron Heffron, president of Market Connections, aimed a question at me even though I was not on the panel. He asked if I was disappointed in where LinkedIn ranked on the effectiveness of channels for Feds (8 out of 12 with a rank of 47%. For SLED it was 22 points higher). I fudged and said no. There are times when I wish I could think faster and come out with the perfect answer, but that was one of those times when I just wasn't prepared.

A more accurate answer now would be, that especially during the pandemic, many more people have been looking to LinkedIn as a major source of content. It also plays a broader role in GovCon than just content delivery. It's a mega-community with thousands of micro-communities in the forms of both personal networks and "groups." It's the first place I go after a briefing like that to connect with those I've just met and to say "hello" to those that I'm connected with but have not physically met, people such as Anna Easterbrook of Carahsoft, who was kind enough to say hello at the briefing.

What LinkedIn brings to the table is:

- Your ability to find and follow 2.2 million feds and who knows how many contractors. Many of these people will connect.

- The networking and building your own network.
- Positioning and branding for individuals and companies.
- The ability to both post and create content. And more.

LinkedIn aside, there is lots of data here showing the overall value of content marketing throughout Fed/SLED, emphasizing once again that those not using content marketing aren't differentiating themselves in ways that resonate across the market.

The one comment from the presentation that resonated deeply with me was from panelist Patricia Davis-Muffett of Amazon Web Services, who remarked that "content is the foundation of Amazon marketing."

Amen!

Essential capture plan components

I developed a streamlined capture planning process based on my experiences as a BD executive. I then implemented it in numerous contractors and in the GovFlex.com Academy. – Mike

Too few of the many government contractors I've worked with have managed to institutionalize the development of new business and recompete capture plans. For more complex, larger procurements, I believe a plan is an indispensable means of gathering and sharing important bid information. A solid capture plan informs the business development process and ensures that no key element is missing. A good capture plan:

- Focuses thinking
- Provides discipline
- Surfaces action items
- Raises win probability
- Provides a framework for capture planning discussions

My experience has been that a Capture Plan is best recorded using Microsoft PowerPoint to avoid unnecessary wordsmithing and to facilitate discussion. It should be a living document. As such, it should be updated regularly to reflect the current pursuit status and to make sure important aspects of the plan aren't ignored.

The first section of the Capture Plan is an examination of the business development information that was collected about the customer (This includes an assessment of the buying influences, including:

- Roles
- Degree of influence
- View of Our Company (green, yellow, red)
- View of Our Company solution (green, yellow, red)
- Price sensitivity and history

The second section presents:

- Competition – who are they; who's teaming together; strengths and red flags
- Company's strengths, weaknesses, weaknesses and red flags
- Technical solution (to include next five bullets)
- Management approach (teammates, subcontract management, organization, corporate resources, performance metrics, deliverables, transition, etc.)
- Project schedule
- Personnel (project manager and other key personnel)
- Past performance (relevance to requirements, on schedule, under budget, client satisfaction, awards, etc.)
- Pricing strategy (scope of the project)
- Price-to-Win (PTW) -- the price which when integrated into the Government's source selection process results in a winning bid (single award or multiple award)
- Proposal team, proposal schedule, Bid and Proposal (B&P) budget requirements
- Major win themes and discriminators
- Action plan for moving forward

The Capture Manager (or Opportunity Lead) should present the capture plan at a planning meeting. After the capture plan discussion, the capture manager should walk through the bid decision elements in the lead tracking system, a PowerPoint Presentation or using an excel or Word table. A bid decision should then be made, or additional action items assigned.

The following sections describe several of the major elements of a Capture Plan in more detail.

Project requirements. To assess a contractor's win probability and to submit a credible, competitive bid, a capture team needs to understand the opportunity program requirements as early in the process as possible. Demonstrating a clear understanding of the requirements informs the management, technical, and cost approach. Establishing the "right" requirements perspective is an iterative process.

First, establish a baseline understanding and then refine that perspective through additional business development activities. Key requirements are those that are most important to solving the customer's problem. Because not all requirements are created equal, the secret to understanding the customer's explicit and implicit requirements is to identify which requirements are most important to the customer and doing so will drive a successful capture solution and proposal. The ideal situation is to be able to relate the key requirements to the acquisition evaluation criteria.

The best way to ensure none of the request for proposal requirements are missed is to collect them in a Requirements Compliance. Prior to an RFP release, this matrix can be used simply as a convenient place to collect the requirements, if known at that time.

At a minimum, this matrix should identify every RFP requirement by number, provide a few words of description and, once the draft or final RFP is released and a decision to bid has been made, address the section in the proposal where that requirement will be discussed.

Many clients request this matrix as part of their proposal activities to help them perform a compliance check. Consider including a matrix like this in your next proposal unless the proposal is too constrained by page numbers. Whether to present the matrix at the beginning of the proposal or to breaking it into sections is a proposal manager's judgment call.

There are many instances where the Statement of Work (SOW) is inconsistent with the proposal instructions and evaluation criteria. How to respond to these situations is also up to the proposal manager. But avoid spending too many hours deliberating the approach. Rather, make sure to provide the evaluator a clear traceability path for purposes of proposal evaluation.

Too many proposal teams get caught up with putting together their approach to the job and lose sight that the first gate they must get through is submitting a compliant proposal. As far as the government is concerned, a non-compliant proposal is just one less bid to factor into the competitive range.

During a capture planning review meeting, share with management how well the capture team understands the customer's requirements. Do they have a solid grasp, a general understanding or do they lack familiarity with the requirements? Identify any actions necessary to strengthen their understanding of the requirements.

Customer relationship. Your company's prior and current customer relationship is a key factor to explore in an opportunity Capture Plan. It is the customer's evaluation of your management, technical, and cost proposals that determines the award outcome. While it is important to maintain good relationships with all individuals capable of influencing the award outcome, it is also crucial that you understand what the customer is thinking and propose a solution that is consistent with their thinking. In the case of negative past performance, some damage control might have to be done to rebuild a positive relationship.

During the procurement process, there might be several people and organizations with the ability to influence the award. The most obvious is the individual or organization within the customer group that will receive the proposed products or services. Others such as superiors, peers and supporting organizations also can affect the award. In many cases, clients will have their own understanding of the problem, the key requirements, the evaluation criteria, and the components of a successful solution.

Where possible, activities should be undertaken to influence the customer positively and ethically prior to the release of a request for proposal. Actions should be taken to:

- Establish strong relationships with all key customer decision makers and influencers
- Demonstrate technical insight
- Get the project manager & technical experts wanted by the customer
- Form the right team of subcontractors

- Develop and communicate a creative, workable solution to the customer's problems
- Influence the SOW with your company's discriminators through white papers, client visits, qualification statements, unsolicited proposals, and technical briefings

It is important to make an honest assessment of how strong your company's relationship is with a target customer. It doesn't mean you might not proceed with a bid. It does give an indication of how much ground you will have to cover in the proposal and allows you to consider actions to be taken to improve customer rapport like teaming with a strong incumbent or hiring a well-liked project manager.

Competition. The competitive landscape is comprised of all companies that are likely to bid on an opportunity. Identifying these companies and how you have performed against them in the past is crucial for your overall capture strategy. Meetings with existing agency contractors as well as previous bidder lists, and award announcements are good starting points for understanding the competitive landscape.

- Identify all the companies that you believe might or will bid on this opportunity.
- Gather any marketing intelligence that will help you to understand each potential competitor's strengths and weaknesses. Sources for this include meetings with all the key industry players, assessment of contract documents such as award fee write-ups, and meetings with the customer.
- Use high, medium, and low or a numerical scale to rate each company or team's relevant competitive strength.

- Ask yourself how you can offset their strengths and take advantage of their weaknesses or maybe even team with a strong competitor to eliminate the competition.

Assess whether the procurement is wired for you, or it is an open competition, or the competition is very strong or unknown. There are many services bids that only require the contractor to provide rates for several labor categories. You might decide that spending time analyzing the competition is not a valuable use of your company's time. However, in almost all cases it is a very important part of the Capture Plan. It should also weigh heavily in the final decision.

Teaming. Here are ten guidelines for successful teaming on competitive procurements.

1. Your company's technical role and work percentage should be clearly defined in a written teaming agreement. Avoid terms like "best efforts" or "goals." These rarely pan out.
2. While established relationships often influence teaming decisions, business associates can be re-assigned or leave their company. Having a definitive teaming agreement is one of the few ways you can mitigate this risk.
3. It is a good practice to request a Dun & Bradstreet credit report on a potential small business prime contractor to assess whether they will be deemed financially credible in the eyes of the client and can pay their bills after contract award.
4. Ask the client what they think of potential teammates – the worst that can happen is they'll decline to comment.
5. Most acquisitions require either the prime contractor or the entire team to provide a certain number of project

citations. Confirm that the prime has the necessary past performance and relevant projects to cite in the proposal.
6. Look for companies that have subject matter experts who can be key personnel in the proposal.
7. Many government acquisitions assume the winning team will hire some or all the incumbent contractor's staff. This will need to be considered as part of your teaming and win strategy.
8. Make sure a potential prime contractor can develop a professional winning proposal.
9. Discuss pricing strategy up front so you know whether the prices you will have to bid will fit within your company's pricing model.
10. Avoid companies that have a reputation for treating their subcontractors unfairly.

On the next page is a decision matrix that can be used to evaluate the teaming landscape for a specific new business opportunity. First, develop the winning criteria (column 1) for subcontractor (teammate) or prime contractor before selecting teammates. These criteria should be based on both stated and perceived client needs as a result of client discussions and reading procurement documentation.

Next assess your own company's ability to meet the key win strategy criteria and any gaps you need to fill with teammates (column 2). Then, evaluate each candidate company against the same criteria using high, medium, or low or a numerical score to determine the best fit (columns 3 – 6).

Win Strategy Criteria	Your Company	Company A	Company B	Company C	Company D
Technical Capability #1	H	H	L	M	M
Technical Capability #2	M	H	H	M	H
Key Personnel	H	M	H	M	H
Past Performance	M	L	H	H	M
Cost Competitiveness	H	L	H	M	H
Potential Teammate?	n/a	No	Yes	No	No

As shown in the competitor columns, it appears that Company A has either high indirect costs or high labor costs based on their low ranking in Cost Competitiveness. Company C lacks the necessary depth in Technical Capability #2 to be of any value to Your Company. Company B and Company D might be good teaming candidates. However, Company B was the first choice they didn't overlap with the prime contractor's core capability as much as Company D and, although not apparent from this matrix, they fulfilled a socio-economic set-aside requirement and were a great future strategic partner.

Once you've agreed to team with a company, make sure you develop effective SOWs for the areas to be subcontracted out. And above all -- avoid teaming just because it's someone you already know...team to win!

The lyrics to a well-known Rolling Stones song -- *"You don't always get what you want"* -- fit my experience with teaming on competitive bids. I once participated as a strategic subcontractor on eleven bids with a large integrator. The small business I worked for was selected because of our strong incumbency in the prime contractor's target agencies. Our team was awarded eight of these eleven contracts, but my company only received actual work on two. It was a painful lesson about knowing which companies have a reputation for treating their subcontractors fairly – especially on professional services contractors.

It's also very important to get your company's technical role and work percentage clearly defined in writing in a teaming agreement. This is often documented in an Exhibit A to the document. The work percentage should reflect a specific percentage or number of staff. Avoid agreements that promise "best efforts" or "goals." These rarely pan out.

In this case, the eight subcontracts that were finally negotiated were not consistent with what was in the teaming agreements. And, because my company didn't have any other relationships with the integrator, there was no one willing to intercede on their behalf.

I learned the hard way that it is very important to get your company's technical role and work percentage clearly defined in writing in a teaming agreement. This is often documented in an Exhibit A to the agreement. The work percentage should reflect a specific percentage or number of staff. Avoid agreements that promise "best efforts" or "goals." These rarely pan out.

Remember – "If you try, sometimes you might find you get what you need!"

Management approach. In best-value procurements, management capabilities and approach are often one the two highest weighted evaluation criteria. The management approach is your company's ability to plan, implement, control, measure, and report on the required work.

An effective management approach should clearly communicate that the selected approach is relevant to the customer's needs. The effectiveness of this approach should have been proven on programs that have similar requirements.

Most services procurements specify a certain number of key personnel or require you to identify who you believe the key personnel should be. It might also be one of the key evaluation criteria. Careful attention should be given to the identification of these individuals and making sure they have strong prior management experience on projects of similar size and scope.

Bidders are also required to prove their ability to staff the project. Your staffing strategy may be to hire the incumbent contractor's staff or to staff a project with your own skilled employees from other projects. It can be quite helpful to involve someone from recruiting and human resources in the discussions for this factor.

Formulate a mitigation strategy for each of the major management risks that might have a significant impact on project schedule, work content or cost. Finally, identify your team's management and capabilities substantiated themes and discriminators.

The key question to be answered is how strong is your management approach and capability? Does your team have the necessary management tools, controls, and metrics for this type of contract?

Technical approach. Your team's technical approach to performing this project should be summarized in this section. It should satisfy the customer's technical requirements and be related to your company's past performance on similar projects.

Provide a high-level view of the major technical requirements. This can be accomplished as a bulletized list, table, flow diagram or a work breakdown structure (WBS) diagram.

Where applicable, the technical approach should clearly identify the necessary tasks and should be used to develop schedules, cost estimates, skill sets, and project risks.

If possible, a project schedule should be developed prior to award. It should be consistent with RFP requirements and the major elements of the management and technical approach. It can help management to visualize the key tasks and deliverables.

Most projects have some degree of infrastructure requirements that may or may not impact pricing. Describe the necessary labor categories and whether current team employees, incumbent hires or new hires will fill these positions.

Also:

- Are there any wage determination requirements to be considered?
- What are the major technical labor categories?
- Will you use in-house people? *(Who, What Organization, What Location)*

- Will you need to hire? (*How Many & When Needed*)

Identify the major technical risks and a brief description of your mitigation strategy.

Substantiated technical themes and discriminators should be communicated to illustrate the relative strength of your team's offering.
Assess your team's ability to meet the technical requirements. Are your approach, staff, and methodologies unique, merely acceptable, or weak in one or more areas?

Past performance. There are at least two main elements of past performance. One is whether your company or team has the required number of project citations that are similar in work type and scope. The second is the quality of performance on these contracts.

First describe the major past performance requirements that fit this opportunity and then identify your team's relevant project references. This can be done as bullets or in a table.

List any past performance that might receive negative client performance feedback. Describe the steps to be taken to mitigate these references prior to proposal submittal.

Assess your team's past performance in terms of the quantity and quality of required past performance references. Does your past performance substantiate your team's ability to perform on the contract?

Here are a few additional guidelines to help raise your evaluation score.

- Select projects that are relevant to the current request for proposal.
- Verify that the former client is willing to provide a positive performance review, and that you haven't recently overburdened them with similar requests.
- If the past performance was negative and you want to include it anyway, you should indicate the corrective action that was taken to fix the problem.
- It is a good idea to notify former clients that you have included them as past performances references.
- Obtain current contact information for the contracting officer or other point of contact to include in your project summary write-up. Also, verify the accuracy of the information being presented. Don't indicate Oracle DB experience when it was SAP.

How GovCon executives should use LinkedIn

Your potential customers are on LinkedIn; you need to be there too. – Mark

In 2010, GSA negotiated with social networks about how those networks could use federal employee data. Since then, LinkedIn has slowly emerged as the dominant network not just in B2B, but also in B2G. LinkedIn is now an integral part of the GovCon ecosystem. Which leads me to why and how CEOs should be participating. Though some executives persist in the notion that Feds are either not on or don't use social media, the evidence is entirely to the contrary.

Having chronicled marketing to the government for 36 years, in two books, 100+ articles in Washington Technology, hundreds of public presentations, and fifteen years of weekly radio shows, I can safely state that We're now neck deep in an era defined and driven by web 2.0 tools and tactics, and in the middle of that is LinkedIn.

Those companies and executives that utilize how LinkedIn can help them communicate with the market are the ones whose companies go further and go faster. Those lacking the ability, time, or motivation to fully leverage the platform are doomed to lag.

There are many examples of executives who lead their companies by posting thought provoking articles that help shape the thinking around specific topics. Dan Helfrich, Chairman and CEO of Deloitte, posts great articles and videos around subjects that are core to what Deloitte offers. He is committed to the thought leadership Deloitte brings to each market segment it serves and he demonstrates this through these posts. His BD people can point to these posts when speaking with federal program managers to show that "top down" commitment.

Several years ago, I wrote about *What Do CEOs Risk by Ignoring LinkedIn? The answer was and still is Plenty.* I outlined some of the benefits for CEOs and other executives to engage on LinkedIn, including:

- Creating higher visibility for your company in a targeted community
- A stronger company brand
- A clear message on what your company offers
- Stronger and deep relationships with current clients and prospects
- Easier access to new accounts
- Better relationships with partners and suppliers
- More GovCon media visibility
- More credibility as a defined niche

Since then, many CEOs and other executives have seen the value of engaging on LinkedIn by posting articles, connecting to peers, key clients, and prospects, and even by endorsing or recommending key people in their companies and at client agencies.

However, there remains a significant percentage of executives from the CEO down who do almost nothing or less to support their company, their staff, or their programs on LinkedIn. They often have profiles with little or no description of who the executive is or what the company does. And this reflects an indifferent attitude to the market. So, if for some reason you harbor the notion that Feds don't use LinkedIn, think again.

Seize the future with we-government

First published in Federal Computer Week in 2004 and then as a chapter in my book, The Enlightened Manager, I think this is a sentiment worth repeating. — Mike

During a speech at the Building a Culture of Peace for the Children of the World exhibit in the Rayburn House Office Building, Rep. Sheila Jackson Lee (D-Texas) encouraged staffers to be more than just members of a group but instead to live and work with a sense of mission. When I heard this, I couldn't help but reflect on how relevant this was to the role of a manager in government or industry.

Real leaders, I had been taught, should play to win and not just to finish. Yet how many workers put in the minimum required effort with the expectation that life doesn't begin until they leave work? How much richer would our lives be if we worked together with a sense of mission, a realization that what we do each day makes a difference in the world and to the future?

If we don't transcend technology with a strong sense of purpose, who will? We each have a choice. We can reluctantly work on tax modernization or fingerprint identification or e-government portals with the feeling that We're just another cog in a technology wheel.

But what would happen if even one manager became determined to create harmony on a project team? If he or she saw the positive potential in each team member? Helped someone uncover her unique contribution to system success? Replaced blame and judgment with hope and initiative? Chose a mission that went beyond just financial or career advancement?

We're all born members of one giant club: humanity. Eventually, we find ourselves constituents of many other smaller groups. The most important choice we make every morning is whether we transcend being passive members and take leadership roles. We've learned that technology by itself can't make the world a better place. But committed managers can.

This means not giving up when faced with seemingly insurmountable obstacles. Budget reductions, abusive bosses, organizational bureaucracy -- all these things can easily reduce us to blithering masses of emotional jelly. So, what can we latch onto in these dark moments?

Lee had it right -- it's the realization that we have a mission in this world. Our children are counting on us to get it right. Let's give we-government a chance. It may be our only hope.

Numbers don't lie: Feds are on LinkedIn

I've been writing about feds on LinkedIn since 2009. – Mark

Long-time readers of my articles and posts know that I've been advocating for the use of LinkedIn in GovCon for over a decade. During that time, many have commented that they didn't believe Feds were on LinkedIn and even if there were "some," they weren't active or interested in connecting with contractors.

I knew Feds were on LinkedIn based simply on how many were connected to me, so about five years ago, I took my first "census" of Feds on LinkedIn, tracking them down by department, agency, operating division – any cluster I could find where they were listed on a LinkedIn "company" page, which allowed me to count how many employees were on LinkedIn.

My first census, back in 2016, showed about 1.8 million federal employees on LinkedIn, representing every federal agency, including the intelligence community.

Now I do the census every year. Between early December 2020 and Jan. 4, I identified LinkedIn "company" pages that represent **305 distinct federal operating organizations**, from cabinet department and their operating divisions, all the military I could identify, and the independent agencies.

This year's total is *2,028,781*. This is a fluid number, as it changes when people update their profiles. Here are some highlights.

Total for DOD and military: 1,121,085

US Army (total 36 "company" pages): 499,474
US Air Force (13 "company" pages): 267, 540
US Navy (26 "company" pages): 251,228
US Marines: 41,587
US Space Force: 910

DoD: (44 "company" pages): 110,346

Total for civilian agencies: 908,869

USDA (12 "company" pages): 49,464
Commerce (12 "company" pages): 35,956
Energy (14 "company" pages): 59,457
HHS (19 "company" pages): 84,598
DHS (11"company" pages): 97,113
Interior (10 "company" pages): 37,033
Justice (11 "company" pages): 37,144
Labor (3 "company" pages): 9,235
NASA (6 "company" pages): 51,506
State: 27,206
DOT (9 "company" pages): 33,973
Treasury (8 "company" pages): 41,523
VA (3 "company" pages): 136,573

Are Feds any more or less active on LinkedIn than contractors? Simple answer is some are, and some aren't. I know too many contractors that are still not active.

I'm personally connected to over 350 Feds, from senior level down to front line PMs. Having been a GovCon marketing advisor for the past 35 years, I find LinkedIn to be the absolute best venue for building and maintaining a relationship-based network. It doesn't replace associations like AFCEA, ACT-IAC or PSC, but it does allow you to do much more with the people in your network, and those with whom you share LinkedIn groups.

When done well, your ability to deploy social selling tactics to supplement your traditional sales and business development efforts should allow you to better penetrate current accounts and expand your influence within those accounts. I've advised many contractors on how to better utilize LinkedIn and continue to monitor the success of many of them.

I joined LinkedIn in early 2004 and my co-author, Mike, has been on LinkedIn since 2007. Both our observations over the past few years tell us that while many in the contracting community are on LinkedIn and use it regularly, most still don't fully grasp the value of the platform.

Do I practice what I preach? Check me out at: www.linkedin.com/in/markamtower.

Maybe a good New Year's "resolution" would be to better leverage LinkedIn. And no, they don't pay me.

Stay in your target market

I've had the misfortune to work for some easily distracted small business owners. It's not always a pretty sight! – Mike

Most small business owners, by their very nature, are agile entrepreneurs at heart. This means they rarely have an idea that isn't worth pursuing. Some of these new business ventures are the reason they have been successful. But most of their companies barely have the bandwidth to maintain and grow business with their current clients much less deal with all the aspects of a penetrating a brand-new market. The impact of LPTA bids has only served to exacerbate this reality.

I've known many companies that have pursued international, software development or commercial opportunities without the staying power, resources, or knowledge necessary to win and deliver these projects. The result is almost always an increase in indirect staff frustration and a decrease in core business revenue.

This is another reason that it is so important for companies to have a solid roadmap of their strategic envelope – the target competencies, services, and customers – where a company is going and how to get there. This helps identify which opportunities should be pursued and, more importantly, which ones should be avoided. Business owners need to remember that business they may want to chase in their minds might not be worth winning in the real world because of the pursuit and operations costs and the negative impact on core business development activities.

A company's adherence to a key set of core competencies and clients is necessary to sustain continued growth. Frequent digressions don't raise win probabilities. So, be careful what you put in your business envelope!

Social selling fiscal end - COVID & beyond

With everyone isolated during the pandemic, I felt compelled to share some of the most effective social selling fiscal year end practices. – Mark

The pandemic has shut down many of the traditional face-to-face end-of-fiscal year venues for sales and business development people. More frequently they are now turning to social networks, especially LinkedIn.

To help you make your time on LinkedIn more productive, here are a few social selling tips. Keep in mind social selling works best when you profile is optimized and tells your viewers what you do, who you do it for and how they can reach you. There is much more to profile optimization but those are the basics.

Social selling is not traditional selling, and it has no elements of a "hard" sell. It's a series of soft touches designed to keep you on the radar of key players in your niche. You know who you need to reach and influence, and you should be able to identify them on LinkedIn.

If you're looking at a particular agency or operating division, you should be able to find up as a "Company" on LinkedIn. Let's use the Defense Health Agency as an example. Look it up on LinkedIn and you'll see the logo in the background section, the number of employees on LinkedIn, and if you have any connections at DHA, right above the employee number you will see how many 1st degree connections you have.

Click on the "See all 1,507 employees" and you go to a page with ten names, photos (if they have one), job title, and if you're a 2nd degree, the number of connections you share with each. The 1,507 represents a 10% growth from my January 2020 Fed LinkedIn census, when there were 1,372 DHA employees on LinkedIn.

On the top navigation bar, you have three other options to refine your search: Connections, Locations and All Filters.

I use the "All Filters" option which takes you to a page with other options, more if you have a paid LinkedIn membership.

Even without a paid membership you can use my two favorite options: location and job title. Using the location for Denver, I find seventy-seven DHA employees. Adding the job title and looking for "IT," I narrow it down to three. If I change it to San Antonio, I get three-hundred and thirty employees and twenty-eight with IT job functions.

If these are people you need to know, the first thing to do is to "Follow" each of them. When you follow someone on LinkedIn, they will be notified via their "Notification" page.

Viewing their profile is touch #1, "Following" is touch #2.

If you share enough 2nd degree connections with some of them, that may be enough of a reason to reach out and connect, but don't send the "LinkedIn form letter."

Use something like this instead. "John, we share, eleven connections at DHA. I have been working with your agency for nearly three years. I would welcome connecting with you."

If some of your shared connections with "John" are industry and not Feds, the odds are much better of getting a connection.

If you focus on a particular agency, posting information about that agency on your profile is a great way to demonstrate your interest. Set up a Google Alert for your agency (spelled out, not the acronym) and monitor the Google feed for articles or blog posts that would be of interest to your prospects. If the article or post has the LinkedIn "share" feature, posting is simple: click on the link, select "share as a post" and add a few comments. Point out what you found useful in the article or perhaps something left out.

If you find an article that mentions key players in the agency, hash tag both the agency and the people. This will increase views for your post.

Your activity, including finding prospects and sharing information, should increase your profile views from those you want to reach.

There are many social selling tactics, but the ones described above can help generate end-of-FY traction.

Make your marketing dollars count

This article which became a chapter in Winning and Managing Government Projects *was written over ten years ago. Still highly relevant but missing some key platforms like LinkedIn and Facebook. – Mike*

Even with the move to more commercial practices, government agency acquisitions are very different from those in industry. However, companies who sell to the government still need to differentiate themselves from their competitors. Government buyers are very sophisticated and expect their suppliers to be able to articulate how their solutions meet unique agency challenges and program requirements. This takes professional branding and marketing material as well as active participation in relevant industry and government associations and conferences.

One of the biggest problems I encountered as a management consultant is organizations that dive into marketing tactics before clearly understanding their overall mission, objectives, and marketing strategy. It is crucial to take the time to make sure you understand the target government market that best fits your product or service. This will accomplish at least two important objectives: (1) encourage you to say "no" to non-core goods or services and incompatible agencies and (2) ensure you select the most cost-effective marketing mix to achieve your objectives. It's all about focus and return on investment.

Several effective government marketing and public relations tactics are described in the following paragraphs. However, the optimal mix of these marketing elements will depend on the company's specific objectives and market.

- Networking at association and local government events (low $ expense/high return on investment (ROI)). A very effective way to meet potential teaming partners and potential government buyers.
- Telemarketing for near term lead generation (medium $/high short-term ROI). Acquire outside support for lead identification/cold calls. There are companies who will take your script for a service or solution and call into target agencies to identify interested government managers to then visit. This is a way to leverage outside resources to supplement a limited inside sales capability.
- Inside sales support – more feet on the street (high $/high short-term ROI). Consider hiring an experienced mid-level task order sales associate to physically sell into targeted government agencies or a lower-level sales associate to telemarket into agencies to generate leads for senior staff follow-up.
- Advertising for near term lead generation. Implement a cost-effective annual advertising plan that focuses on the highest ROI solution/service. Target federal or state and local trade magazines with the intention of generating click-thru's to your company's Web site. Advertising alternative analysis:
- Print (high $/low ROI): Magazine print advertising can be prohibitively expense for small companies. To be effective, at least 4-6 ads need to run per year. Also, print ads rarely generate real leads but rather brand recognition or end of fiscal year purchase influence for product sales. This is probably only appropriate if your company has the revenue to support the overhead expense. Print advertising is an effective way to introduce a new product launch or to build brand awareness.

- Online (medium $/medium to high ROI short term): Online trade newsletter advertising can be more affordable. For instance, your company could sponsor a trade magazine newsletter for a two-month period and measure click-thru rates and lead generation.
- Company email newsletter (low $/low ROI short term). A company permission-based email newsletter, maybe quarterly, can generate a lot of recognition. Might be worth exploring. There are quite a few online services that aren't that expensive. Remember to make it permission based.
- Conference sponsorship and panel participation (low to medium $/medium ROI). Make sure to target conferences to actively participate in that attract your company's most likely prospects. Try to get a senior company executive on the conference advisory board and/or as a speaker. Sign up as a sponsor for maximum exposure (if affordable).

Does traditional PR still matter?

I last wrote about the current state of PR in 2018. – Mark

GovCon trade publications have morphed from robust hardcopy magazines in the late 1990s through the mid-2000s to online hubs featuring news, events, and more for our community. Broadcast media still owns the airwaves but are also supported by robust web sites.

One question I get via email with some regularity is, "So if it's not a hardcopy magazine, is it still valuable? Should I spend my time, and perhaps money, to get into one of the online trade publications?" We get on the phone and the conversation goes something like this:

Them: It seems so many companies have blogs and e-newsletters. Should I start a newsletter, or should I try to get interviewed by *Washington Technology*?

Me: There is no one size fits all answer, but if the publication serves your market, and the article you want to be in or write targets a sweet spot for your business, the answer is probably yes.

Them: But what if I publish a blog, start a newsletter, or post on LinkedIn?

Me: What kind of traffic does your blog get, and how many views do you average on LinkedIn?

Them: But I've heard you say quality is better than quantity.

Me: True, but you need traffic before either can occur. Traditional media, print and broadcast, have the traffic. Most company blogs and newsletters don't. And if they do, it didn't happen overnight.

Them: So, what are you saying?

Me: Ask yourself:

- Why you want to be in the media?
- Why would the audience served by the media outlet want to hear what you say?
- How this would this exposure benefit your company?
- Do you need help getting interviewed?
- Is it worth the time and potential expense?

Them: That's a lot to absorb. I'll have to think about it.

Me: Think hard and understand what you want out of being in any media. The bottom line is that when journalists want an informed opinion, they go to a trusted source, someone known in the market. The media wants to hear from experts. If not you, who?

By the way, when it comes to my clients, I prefer for them to be quoted rather than their competitor, and I prefer it to occur in a significant media outlet.

Line staff need to talk about growth

This became a chapter in a company's project management handbook in 1998 and is still entirely relevant today.

What strategies can you employ to give your staff the confidence to discuss organic business growth with their government clients?

Each organizational unit is comprised of staff with a range of behavioral characteristics. Some take to business development like a duck to water; others would rather have a root canal than talk to their clients about future requirements. The challenge for the manager is to channel the efforts of the more aggressive staff and coach the reluctant ones.

Techniques that have worked for my consulting clients include incorporating business growth initiatives as an integral part of the annual review and career growth planning process. This helps the staff member to correlate helping grow the business with personal reward and growth. It is also helpful to do some client visits together with the employee so they can see how it is done (and that it isn't as painful as they might have imagined)!

I had one client implement a client visit contest. Project managers and BD staff participated but with different goals. The BD professional and the project manager with the most in-person growth related discussions with current or prospective clients in each month received a cash bonus. The company went from about 3-4 visits a month to over 25! Totally changed their culture.

Having said all that, I think it is important to accept that some people will just never get with the program and to push them will only result in mutually assured destruction! Either because they don't agree with it, or they're just not wired for it. Which is okay -- we all have our role to play!

The simple act of being on LinkedIn is marketing

In his seminal essay "Marketing is Everything" in the Harvard Business Review (January 1991), Silicon Valley legend Regis McKenna makes the case that technology changed the face of marketing. Twenty-nine years later, that message still resonates. – Mark

Marketing occurs with every action, or inaction, in our business lives. It occurs when we attend business events, have a one-on-one with co-workers, clients, or partners, and when we engage via social media. Each action creates an impression of who you are, what you do and how you act. And, most important, you get to live with the results. Everything you do defines something about you and in turn, reflects on your company.

LinkedIn is your major face-forward to the market. It's where people will vet you and your company, looking to see who You are and what you do. Often, it's the first impression someone has of you, so it better be good.

Seven years ago, I wrote the first version of "*The Simple Act of Being on LinkedIn is Marketing.*" That post's message was transparent: simply being on LinkedIn is marketing yourself and representing your company. You control the content, who you connect with, the groups you join, the information you share- or don't share. It's all there, and you're in control.

While there is nothing earth-shattering about that statement, its simplicity belies its importance. This is why I'm incredulous that so many people seem to be so cavalier about how they present themselves on LinkedIn, what they post (if anything) and the message(s) that sends.

So many people simply cut-and-paste from their resumes, or worse, leave entire sections blank.

You don't need a Premium account to stand out on LinkedIn, so you can market yourself. **It's free.**

You can highlight your unique skills, knowledge, relationships and more. **It's free.**

You can build a network of your associates, partners, prospects, and clients. **It's free.**

You can add graphics, videos, presentations, posts and more. **It's free, too!**

In the 11+ years I've been coaching people on LinkedIn, I've viewed thousands of profiles, including the "bones in the desert" approach (minimal or no information on your profile), the snarky approach with a cartoon character or famous person for your photo, and many more. I often use these in my presentations on how <u>not</u> to present yourself.

Then there are those who use LinkedIn to take political or other non-business-related stands which, given the political climate, are often quite negative. Certain behavior is just not acceptable in a business setting, and if you don't understand that, I don't want you in my network. So, please take the high road.

LinkedIn affords you the best opportunity to present yourself in a positive way to your market segment. It does require some serious thought before putting pen to paper, or more precisely, fingers to keyboard, but the results are worth it.

In a relationship-driven market like GovCon, every impression you make is marketing, and it needs to be great. **For both yourself and the company you work for, the simple act of being on LinkedIn is marketing**. Not taking full advantage of LinkedIn means more business for your competition.

Turn budget fear into opportunity

Seems like every generation suffers through at least one or two economic downturns which afford me the opportunity to write about them! – Mike

According to news feeds and LinkedIn discussions, the sky is falling exclaimed Chicken Little at the end of yet another dismal sales pipeline review. His business development executive responded, *"When's the last time we really sat down and talked to our customers? I mean are they even buying what we're selling?"* Mr. Little was stumped.

Like Chicken, my daily industry news alerts are filled with gloom and doom – pessimistic forecasts about the economy, the budget, and the devastating impact on federal agencies and government contractors.

Having spent over 40+ years in our market, I have been through several major slowdowns, shutdowns, and turnarounds. And while this one is multi-dimensional and particularly insidious, it is a good time to remember that the lotus flower blooms in the muddy swamp.

With this constructive attitude, successful companies will take advantage of the current situation to retool their services and strategic focus to align with the most likely funded programs and agencies. The result will be a higher win rate and increased revenue. No one said this would be easy. But, if it were, I'd still be doing it!

When times get tough like this, business developers (and executives) often respond by desperately trying to push their services onto government buyers. This is major turn-off. More than ever, now is a time to work smarter not just harder. This means really listening to your customers, looking for new strategic partnerships and researching your target market. Market analysts research companies excel at helping you match your core competencies with the most attractive agencies and specific federal opportunities.

Epilogue. Unfortunately, Chicken Little was let go.

Seven habits of highly successful LinkedIn networkers

I think it's crucial that professionals understand how LinkedIn has changed over the years. – Mark

In the last 16 years I've been on LinkedIn, it has morphed and re-morphed, added and deleted features and apps, changed layouts, and much more, with virtually no notice to members except for the occasional "after the fact" announcement. LinkedIn guru Andy Foote and others documented no less than 25 changes on LinkedIn in 2019, some good, some bad, and some strange. Here is Andy's list just from 2019:

JAN – Position Grouping
JAN – About (Summary)
FEB – LinkedIn Live
MAR – Photo Tagging
APR – Teammates
APR – Reactions
MAY – Co Page Follow
JUN – LinkedIn Comments
JUN – Interview Prep Videos
AUG – Documents Tab
SEP – Save Feed Content
SEP – Open to Opportunities
SEP – Open for Business
SEP – Featured by LinkedIn Editors
SEP – Find an Expert

SEP – Skill Assessments
OCT – LinkedIn Events
OCT – Find Nearby
OCT – Personalized Invitations (Mobile)
NOV – Indexed Posts
NOV – Visibility of Shared Posts
DEC – Hashtags In URL
DEC – Most Relevant (Top Comments)
DEC – Pending Content (Groups)
DEC – Reply Auto Tag/Mention

By the way, you can find Andy's detailed description of these changes by searching for Andy Foote and 2019 Changes on Linked Insights.

All this being said, LinkedIn remains my absolute favorite GovCon sandbox, providing a venue where you can do extraordinary things "IF" you understand the platform and the rules of the game. Then you can make LinkedIn work for you even when you're offline.

Despite the changes, and with a tip of the hat to Stephen Covey, here are *Seven Habits of Highly Successful (and Visible) LinkedIn Networkers*. Use these well and succeed, because they aren't impacted by the myriad of changes that continue to occur.

1. Determine your goals and develop a plan. To get from point A to point B, you must know what point B is. You may not know *where* it is yet, but you have to know what you want to accomplish by being on LinkedIn. Multiple goals are OK, but you need to write them down and refer

to them as you build your profile, add connections, join groups, and become more active.
2. Develop a great profile. Your goals will determine how you write your profile and what you include. You need to be clear throughout your profile as to who you are, what you do, and what you're looking to accomplish as well as the value you bring to your market niche. Understand that a profile is not a presence (more on this in #5). Use details, short paragraphs (white space), and graphics throughout your profile. When you see things on other profiles that impress you, ask yourself if you can do something similar.
3. With your plan in place and your profile done well, connecting is next. Your plan should indicate the types of people you wish to connect with, the level of person, types of companies, geography of prospects, and more. Your outreach will be more successful *if* your target audience looks at your profile before accepting or rejecting your invitation. Getting them to look at your profile means NOT sending out the LinkedIn connection form letter. People are more likely to respond if you offer a context for wanting to connect. *Offer a reason* when reaching out and have a profile that backs up the reason.
4. Joining pertinent groups is still important, especially if LinkedIn fulfills its promise to bring back some of the best group features. Groups are communities of people who have identified interests in a specific topic, geographic area, technology, business discipline, etc. There are groups for everything. The group profile should make it easy for you to know if a group is right for you. Groups are great for learning, sharing, commenting, asking questions, connecting, and gaining visibility in targeted communities. Group size doesn't matter as much as the makeup of the membership and the group activity. One

perpetual value of groups is being able to scroll through the roster of current members.
5. Activity (aka social selling) is what takes a profile from passive to an active presence on LinkedIn. Sharing information through your profile, group activity, sending items to other LinkedIn members should be the first step. Commenting on other people's posts will take it up a notch. The more active you are, the more visible you become. The more value your content adds, the more credibility you build along the way.
6. Integrate LinkedIn into all your business activities. Have a link to your company profile and individual profiles on your business web site, business card, and any other related marketing collateral. Include your personal LinkedIn URL on your email signature. When you pick up business cards at a networking event, look them up and connect.
7. Review and adjust. Your goals aren't written in stone and will change, sometimes slightly, other times more radically. Adjust your profile, groups, and activities accordingly.
8. Regardless of what changes come down the pike, these seven steps should remain constant and help you succeed.

Just say no to bad bids

15 years ago, when this was written, it was obvious (as it still is now) that successful businesses needed to pay attention to the quality of their sales pipeline. – Mike

A few years ago, I spent a half-day with a small business helping them improve their business development process. However, it soon became apparent that their major challenge to growing to the next level was a lack of definition of what they wanted to be in three years, what their core solutions and competencies were, and which vertical domains they should concentrate on. This led to an animated discussion about their win probability (low), their bid decision making process (weak), their ability to describe their company (vague at best), and their willingness to say no to out-of-bounds pursuits (non-existent). Some of the comments I heard were, "If we submit enough bids, we're bound to win our share," and "I'm afraid to say no to an opportunity because it may be a real game changer." My prescription for this affliction is Gamblers Anonymous!

In general, the most successful companies I've worked with have found an effective balance between too little focus and too much. Unfortunately, for every executive who can inculcate this into their culture, there are many more who have a limited ability to focus. According to my highly statistical calculations (i.e., educated guess), the probability of building a solid, thriving company using a broad shotgun approach to submitting competitive bids is 22.3%. It works for some types of services but is still the exception, not the rule.

This doesn't mean laser precision on everything. Too much rigidity in the development of a bid pipeline will blind the company to new service and agency possibilities. But successful strategic plans shouldn't rely on luck to achieve the desired objectives. When it comes to business growth, the no's usually have it.

LinkedIn's fiscal year end power

This article was my way of taking pity on all the salespeople who I've witnessed chasing end-of-fiscal-year dollars. – Mark

As you move deeper into the summer months, have you considered the ways LinkedIn can help you at the end of the fiscal year? First a few facts, then a few tips.

There are now 2.2 million Feds on LinkedIn, representing *every* federal and DOD agency. Let that sink in: *2.2 million Feds.* The most represented job function on LinkedIn is IT, and the same holds true for Feds. My unscientific research shows 15 percent or more of Feds on LinkedIn have an IT job title or function. That's 330,000 feds.

Do I have your attention yet?

Now for just a few literally tip-of-the-iceberg tips.

The end-of-fiscal year FED purchasing results in increased use of contractual vehicles that are easy to access, especially IDIQs and GWACs. If you own a coveted spot on SEWP V, OASIS, or any other well-used contract, *make sure your sales team mentions these contracts on your LinkedIn profile.* Not mentioning your major contracts on your profile is like showing up at a networking event without your business cards and assuming people will remember you.

The first two questions a Fed will ask are "How does your product or service help me," and then, "How can I buy it."

Without that second part of the equation, they are likely to move on – especially at the end of the fiscal year.

Adding the contract info is simple, right? Now that you have their attention, how can they reach out to you?

Last time I looked there is no "Inquiry" form attached to your profile for people to send info requests, so what are your options? The most obvious option is to have your contact information, phone and/or email, on your profile. Yes, they can always send an InMail, if they have access to InMail, but why not make it easier for them *and include your contact information?*

I've probably heard all the arguments against having contact info on your profile; but I believe making it easy for those you want to connect negates the objections.

How about ABM, account (or agency) based marketing? If you have sales reps who manage specific agency accounts, using LinkedIn to penetrate those accounts more fully should be on your "to-do" list. Look up the agency or operating division as if it were a company and click on the employees. The list shows up immediately.

These are all simple things, right? Yet so few people do them which means leaving money on the table for others to find.

These tactics will work for you even when you're not on LinkedIn. How cool is that?

So, can LinkedIn help at the end of the fiscal year? Yes. And for the rest of the year as well.

When to ask for the sale

I've witnessed so many business developers approach sales in a less than desirable manner that I decided to document some best practices. — Mike

"The human brain starts working the moment you are born and never stops until you stand up to speak." - Sir George Jessen

Identifying new business leads is not too much different from mining for gold. Both require an entrepreneurial spirit, patience, commitment, and some luck. Two of the most critical steps are: (1) to become familiar with the company's products or services and, (2) to be open to what's going on around you by increasing your situational awareness. Both steps are necessary for you to be able to match your capabilities with a potential client's needs.

Regarding situational awareness…50% of new business success involves gaining an understanding of a government manager's needs (Okay…maybe it's 51%). This can be as simple as introducing yourself to government employees in your area who you don't normally meet with to gain a better understanding of their responsibilities and problems. Or, through dialogue you might discover your current client has a new requirement the company can fulfill. Sounds obvious, but it is amazing to me how few industry professionals do this, preferring instead to stay well within their comfort zone. But, faced with a rapidly changing and highly competitive marketplace, playing it safe doesn't usually result in career growth.

Where possible, knowledge collection about a sales prospect should begin before any actual client contact is initiated. Start by identifying the client's organization, mission, and the specific people you should call. Gather relevant information from agency Web sites, news and trade magazine Web sites, agency strategic plans, internal and external agency audit reports and individuals who are familiar with your target prospect. In other words, do your homework.

The purpose of the first visit is to assess a prospect's needs and to establish a personal rapport. First impressions are usually lasting ones. So, find common interests, market your personal qualities, be a good listener and let your enthusiasm show. Be positive. If they talk, listen. Did I remember to say *listen*?

And don't fear rejection. If you experience an anxiety attack at the mere thought of approaching someone you don't know to explore a business relationship, then it might help to view selling as an opportunity to meet new people. I often strike up conversations with people I meet at the grocery store and in the elevator. I consider each encounter a chance to create a bridge between that person and me. What else in life could be more important? You may not want to go to this extreme, but surely this is a worthwhile behavior to apply to your immediate work environment. You might be pleasantly surprised at the personal dividends such actions pay.

Try to be five minutes early. But not so early that you appear to be desperate. Don't pass out sales materials when you want the prospect to focus on you. If you're going to hand out sales materials, try to interact with the materials as opposed to just handing them over. Avoid reading each bullet on your slides. The prospect can read. Rather, make a relevant point about each slide and then solicit a comment or ask a question. Again, your mission is to try to get the prospect talking, and then to match your company's capabilities with their needs.

If you make a corporate overview pitch, keep it as brief as possible. Focus on the prospect's needs instead. Don't feel like you must present every company capability. You're not being graded on quantity! If they don't show an interest in something you're presenting or describing, then change the subject. Watch their body language. They'll let you know how you're doing. If you detect snoring or the sound of a head striking a desktop, then change your direction.

There are least four critical pieces of information I try to discover on every sales call (if the prospect will let me).

- Who are the decision-makers?
- What are the client's needs?
- Does the client have sufficient budget to address the problems they have identified?
- When will the decision-makers be able to make the decision to buy?

During your dialogue, look for how you can help the client. The needs of different agencies vary according to their mission. Some organizations, like the Patent and Trademark Office and the U.S. Mint, are driven by the need for increased revenue generation and customer satisfaction. Intelligence and defense agencies strive for information superiority, improved operations, and enhanced decision support. Most civilian agencies worry about cost management, enhanced information security and maximized return on investment. Almost all potential customers have at least one compelling need...something that is keeping them up at night. Find out what that is and, if you can "scratch their itch," you're on the road to doing business with them.

I find it useful to avoid giving too many direct answers to questions. For instance, if I'm asked, "What's your delivery time?" I respond with, "Is delivery time important to you? What delivery time do you need?" This protects me from giving the "wrong" answer. (Works great at home with significant others as well!)

Anticipate objections. Listen carefully. Try to differentiate your company's services. Explain why your company and your services are better. Sometimes a client's objection is just a misunderstanding of something you said. If they misunderstood – offer more information. If they are skeptical, offer proof. For instance, you might cite an example of how you've helped another client achieve a similar result. Or, if necessary, you can promise to get back to them with proof of the company's experience.

If they identify a drawback of your service (maybe you're more expensive than some other contractor) – minimize the drawback and go back to the big picture, the overwhelming benefits of your service or product. If they mention a real problem with your company – take action. Offer to help eliminate the problem. The main point is not to wait to hear, "I want to think about it," or "I have to ask my supervisor, my spouse, my spiritual advisor." Instead, encourage your prospect to voice their objections so that you can mitigate their concerns.

If you have had a positive interchange and have identified a match between a client problem and a company's solution, then ask for the sale. It's simple. Repeat after me, "What steps do we need to take to move forward to the solutions we've just discussed?" Avoid loaded terms like legal, binding, final and closing. And don't be discouraged if the client then brings up more objections. These can be "buying" signs and don't necessarily mean the client isn't going to contract with you for your products or services.

Establish a follow-up agenda with the prospect. Try to offer something of value such as a technical paper. Express your appreciation later with a thank you message. Remember — if you don't follow-up, someone else will!

Small businesses need to stand out

Acquainting a potential client with your capabilities and past performance rests squarely on each small business. – Mark

Getting on the radar (in a positive way) of government buyers and influencers before you start bidding seems to be a daunting task for some. When I speak at proposal and contracting events, a major complaint from small businesses that lose on bids is "the customer didn't know us."

This is not a problem for the customer, the government agency. It's YOUR problem, and there are several ways to get on the radar of government buyers and influencers, before, during and after the bidding process.

The first method is to go to agency briefings, often held by the agency Office of Small & Disadvantaged Business Utilization and get some face time with the small business office. Industry associations and publications often hold events where feds will speak, and this is another chance to briefly get in front of influencers. The biggest problem with these methods is the company executive often doesn't know how to present him/herself and the company's skill set.

I recently attended the Washington Technology Category Management Industry Day, which had several good presentations. Among the speakers was John Bergin from the Defense Department's CIO office. He mentioned taking lots of meetings with small businesses, most of which would be one-time only, as the company offered no real value during their visit. A phrase Bergin used resonated with me regarding these small companies: "You have to be market differentiated."

For live meetings, Sean Kelley, a federal chief information security officer and president of GITEC offered these thoughts. First, what's the mission of the agency? Second, what are they doing that needs what you bring to the table? Third, how do they access these products or services, what contracts do they use or prefer? If you can't address these before the meeting, you're not ready to meet. Reschedule and do your homework first.

A second method to get on the radar is generating content with possible solutions that addresses a problem the agency (or agencies) face. Recent studies by Hinge Marketing and Market Connections both show that sharing pertinent content with key influencers before and during the buying process, can position your company favorably.

But don't assume emailing a fed your white paper will get it read. Building a position as a trusted source of information is not a one-off process. It's a continuous process, one that helps establish your company as a subject matter expert in a specific area. This is what Bergin was driving at when he said, "You have to be market differentiated."

If you're simply one in a long line of small IT companies meeting with a government executive and you don't emphasize a skill you bring to the table that the executive needs, the likelihood of a second meeting disappears. When you combine these two approaches, you have a much higher likelihood of success.

The simple answer is visibility helps, but *only when it adds credibility* to your company and your subject matter experts. The credibility occurs when you add value to your market *in a*

95

visible and regular way. Differentiate. Demonstrate a competitive advantage that can help the prospect agency, and your chances of success are much higher.

Five habits of incompetent BD executives

I learned my most valuable leadership lessons through my own mistakes and suffering through the mistakes of others. – Mike

Based on over 250 management-coaching assignments, my own experience and an over-stimulated imagination, here are five habits of highly incompetent sales executives (and other leaders) and how to deal with them.

1. **Avoids making decisions.** There is a time to self-reflect and gather information. There is also a time to fish or cut bait. This individual's inability to reach a timely conclusion can drive you crazy and contributes to organizational malaise and low win probabilities. Not unusual for this type of manager to avoid putting anything in writing. Your only solution is to document everything that does and doesn't happen and email it back to them for verification.
2. **Treats staff like personal servants.** Stuck in a bygone era, these managers have an over inflated sense of importance and a lack of respect for subordinates. Their style would work successfully on pirate ships but is not a motivating influence in modern organizations. Best to disconnect your phone to avoid their midnight calls or texts and lock your (virtual) office door to hide from late Friday assignments due on Monday morning. Better yet…lose the Zoom login or move to another state.
3. **Overly politically sensitive.** At the top of this individual's agenda is pleasing upper management. It comes before everything else including making the right decisions. Often collects facts only to ignore them or refuses to listen to bad news. Also has a difficult time staying on target or saying no to bad new business pursuits. Avoids conflict by saying yes to everything

instead of acting as a filter to prevent subordinate burnout. Deal with this manager by regularly presenting a list of your tasks and how many you can accomplish within your resource restraints. Wait for a prioritization or make your own.

4. **Hides true BD pipeline status.** The bane of many government contractors, some managers believe risk avoidance means to only report the news that superiors want to hear. So, win probabilities are always 75% or higher with inflated revenue projections – until they aren't. Then it is time to blame others. The only cure, other than forced backbone implant elective surgery, is to carefully document the correct sales opportunity status and keep on chugging.

5. **Is technically proficient but people impaired.** Beware technical experts with poor BD or people skills. Rather than admit to a lack of management acumen, they accept ever-increasing levels of responsibility without the necessary training. Their compensation and stature are inversely related to the number of subordinates who enjoy working for them. They often wallow in the minute capture details when they should concentrate on the bigger issues and most important bids. Company leaders too often look the other way until the BD strategy implodes and the best BD staff depart for saner pastures. This will be a wonderful learning experience about how not to treat your team members when you get promoted.

By the way, I have a strong aversion to chain emails and social media posts. Especially the ones that say I'll sprout something terrible like a second head unless I forward the message to ten of my friends. Still, I urge you to send this chapter to ten of your neediest business associates – it may be their only hope! As for the head thing – no promises!

Critical questions to ask when seeking outside help

I wrote this article in 2017 after watching several small businesses struggle to adequately screen critical outside help. — Mark

Scenario one: Recently I helped a Fortune 500 company select a federally focused communications firm for a targeted marketing campaign. I reviewed the criteria, the scope of the project, and the potential audience and then selected two firms for the client to review. We received proposals (written and oral) from both, and as I expected, both were very much on target.

Scenario two: My phone rings, I answer. I get a long story about "how my company registered at SAM.gov, got a call a few days later from 'an expert' on all things GSA, signed an agreement, and paid thousands for a GSA Schedule. But now, nothing is happening." Both Mike and I have had over 100 of these calls in the last ten years.

You got a call, were sold a load of BS, you "bought it," and you didn't vet the caller? *Lucy, we gotta problem here...*

In the government contracting world there are service providers for virtually everything: outsourced business development, marketing, sales, capture, and proposal development, bid services, headhunters, obtaining a GSA Schedule, market intel, back-office support, lobbying for your contract, events and event producers, human resources, legal, accounting, insurance, finance and so much more.

There are providers that are excellent in their respective niches. Unfortunately, there are too many generic service providers that claim expertise in B2G predicated on their only knowing a few acronyms. There are also scam artists who prey on those thinking GovCon market entry is simple.

When it comes to selecting outside services, how do you make the choice? What are your criteria?

First and foremost, if you have a decent personal GovCon network, ask around. If a company is good, you should be able to find out. If a company is not so good, you should be able to find out faster. But you will never know until you ask around.

After asking around, here are a few thoughts to help your selection process.

Read about the people and company on LinkedIn. Are the key staff at the company experienced in this market? I've looked at the profiles of some alleged GSA Schedule advisors only to find they were either selling real estate or burgers six months back. Have they been out of the market for several years and are just now coming back in? Endorsements and recommendations on their profiles will help, as will the number of connections you share. I heard one PR firm claim to be the leading PR firm in B2G, only to find they were not connected to any reporters or editors at any of the trade publications.

Referrals from past customers are another way to vet outside services. Admittedly, you will only get people to contact who are likely to be positive but ask hard questions when you speak to them. When did the work occur? What were tangible results? How long did it take? Was it within budget? Ask for more references. References have their own reputations to worry about as well, so most won't be misleading.

Comparison shopping is always a good idea. Have a team on your side review at least three outside services, then brainstorm your results on a (now virtual) white board session discussing the pros and cons for each provider to select the one(s) who make the final cut. But don't be afraid to toss out all the companies reviewed and look for new ones if there is not a solid fit. It's better to have no service provider than a bad one.

Here are a few questions you might want to ask any outside service provider:

- Tell me about yourself and your business.
- What's your approach in working with your clients?
- What's your preferred way to communicate with clients?
- What additional support or services do you provide?
- What are your company's strengths? Weaknesses?
- Who will be my main point of contact and who else will I be working with?
- Tell me about a particular client project (without breaking confidentiality) and the outcomes achieved.

Not all outside service providers are created equal, and size is not an indicator of talent.

Caveat emptor!

How to assess a company's sales health

Not too much has changed since I assembled this checklist in 2000 to my clients (and me) conduct due diligence on potential acquisitions. – Mike

Areas to be looked at when assessing a potential acquisition's business development health, are:

- Copies of all strategic sales/marketing documents or plans
- Historical sales results including number and size of bids; win/loss rate (if available)
- Current business backlog and comparison with historical information
- Growth opportunities – new business projections including all pending bids or proposals
- Market expansion opportunities (if any)
- Technology initiatives and planned investments
- Business/service/client mix including any dependence upon a single or few customers
- Unique capabilities
- Trademarks, patents, copyrights
- Software products
- Client list by size and duration
- Copies of all contracts including contract vehicles and subcontracts
- Identification of all contracts/revenue won through small business or set-aside programs
- Unusual contract clauses
- Labor rate/pricing strategy
- Client relations, reputation and goodwill including past performance (copy of any client satisfaction surveys)

- Channel relations with vendors
- Teaming relations with other small businesses and integrators
- Conflicts of interest that might impact future market growth
- Geographic location of current markets
- Marketing collateral (can it be used by your company)?
- Social media presence
- Web site content and appearance
- Scheduled trade shows, conferences, speaking engagements or advertising commitments
- Business development process documents
- Lead tracking system description and latest lead list
- Proposal capability including resumes and project summaries
- Sales staff including outside consultants
- Company non-compete policy (in effect?)
- Sales incentive/bonus commitments/policies

Social selling changes your bid decisions

I've always said it's almost impossible to win a contract if the customer doesn't know you. – Mark

One of the more recurrent complaints when a company is making the "go/no go" decision on a bid is, "We'll lose because the client doesn't know us." Bob Davis said this the first time I saw him speak in the early 1990s and I've heard it hundreds of times since, especially when I speak at the APMP-NCA fall conference. If this is a common refrain for proposal professionals, it's got to be an issue across the board.

Enter LinkedIn and social selling.

Social what? Social selling is the process of getting on the radar of specific niches within the market you serve and staying there in a non-intrusive way, adding value by sharing content, making intelligent comments on group posts, viewing profiles of influencers, reaching out to your first-degree connections occasionally, and reaching out to connect with new people when the time is right.

Social selling occurs online in social networks, especially LinkedIn.

What social selling isn't, is traditional sales. It's not simply a "close-the-deal" scenario. Social selling is an important adjunct process that helps open doors and keep them open.

Let's start with my favorite GovCon researcher, Market Connections (now part of GovExec) and their 2018 Federal Government Contractor Study. It indicated how contractors rate themselves in the ten areas they deem most important. Of these, eight can leverage social selling techniques. Demonstrating thought leadership and subject matter expertise requires a LinkedIn profile and content that shows that expertise.

While you may not be able to manage each of your government contacts, you can keep them informed about what your company is doing. LinkedIn provides a platform to demonstrate your points of differentiation. Indeed, those points of differentiation often substantiate your thought leadership position.

Capturing and managing customer data is also a function of LinkedIn. You can see where your prospect/customer has worked previously, how long they've been in their current position, and more. This should be helpful when prepping for a sales call.

Sharable content also supports the sales department.

Lead generation can start with looking up the client organization as a company on LinkedIn and using the appropriate search filters to find key people. All Federal agencies and operating divisions have company pages.

Business development and sales staff should be doing all the above to enhance their other BD and sales activities. Moving leads and prospects through the sales funnel starts with these tasks followed by connecting with key influencers and adding them to your network.

A few other things social selling can help you with include:

- Account/agency-based marketing efforts
- Establishing and reinforcing your brand
- Building those oh-so-important relationships

Done well, social selling strengthens the relationship between sales and marketing and makes each more effective.

By engaging in social selling, you can kiss the "the client doesn't know us" syndrome goodbye and make more Yes bid decisions!

Basic labor rate terminology

BD, capture and proposal professionals should be familiar with these key financial terms I wrote about while developing the project management guide for ManTech International.. – Mike

There was a time, as a BD professional, I used to think labor rate terminology was a language, like Greek or Latin, that only finance people spoke. I would nod my head in bid reviews as if I really understood what was being talked about. Eventually, I learned that different organizations, depending on their function and experience, used different terms to refer to labor rates and cost structure. So, for those who are linguistically challenged, here are some very basic terms with their associated meanings that I think are accepted by most:

- A **labor rate** (sometimes called a **direct rate**) is a financial term that describes the hourly rate of a specific type of labor. In federal contracting, this term is often modified by the words *unburdened* or *burdened*.
- An **unburdened labor rate** is the hourly rate being paid to an employee.
- A **burdened labor rate** (sometimes called a **sell rate** or **billable rate**) is the final negotiated hourly labor rate on an approved contract. This rate includes overhead costs, G&A, and fees.
- **General & Administrative** (G&A) expenses are costs incurred by a business because of carrying out day-to-day operations. These are mainly comprised of costs that aren't directly related to project delivery.

- A **wrap rate** is a factor that when multiplied by an hourly labor rate equals the final fully burdened rate minus profit.
- An **operating unit** is a collection of similar work within a definable organizational unit that applies the same wrap rate to hourly labor rates. In other words, an operating unit, sometimes called a **cost center**, has the same overhead & G&A structure.

If these labor rate terms seem like a foreign language to you, please know that you're not alone. Many people, even accountants and financial analysts, struggle with this terminology especially as it relates to federal business development. But time spent getting "labor rate smart" will pay big dividends for both you and your company.

Second, in the heat of the competitive bidding frenzy, it's easy to forget that all government contracts aren't created equal. Some place a greater financial and performance risk on the client and others on the contractor. It's extremely important to know the difference. Here is a very rough overview of this risk continuum in order (low to high) of relative risk to the contractor.

- **Cost-plus fixed fee.** Kind of like investing in certificates of deposit. A lower known profit with no upside potential but minimal financial risk.
- **Cost-plus award fee.** Either some or all the potential profit is awarded based on pre-defined performance criteria. A good deal for reliable companies – not so good for poor performers.
- **Cost-plus incentive fee.** Same protection from overruns but with performance-based fee.

- Time and materials – Depending on how the contract is written, there is the potential for higher profit if you hire and manage to your negotiated labor rates. The opposite is also true.
- **Cost-plus with rate limits.** Something for everyone and, if you ask some people, nothing for anybody!
- **Firm-fixed price level of effort.** I've never had a good experience with the words "firm-fixed price" and labor contracts. Too many variables that can go wrong.
- **Performance based.** Not "officially" a contract type. But very suitable when the government knows what it wants. When it doesn't, this can be a nightmare. Hence it is high on my risk spectrum.
- **Fixed price deliverable.** Depending on the product or service to be delivered, this isn't necessarily risky. But, particularly onerous for system development projects including commercial not-really-off-the-shelf software.

Disclaimer: My experience is no guarantee of future risk or results. Carefully study each Request for Proposal (RFP) Statement of Work, pricing requirements and special clauses.

How to crack the WT Top 100

Ten years ago, I wrote my first column for Washington Technology on how to break into the Washington Technology Top 100. Now it's time to revisit – Mark

Every year when *Washington Technology* publishes the Top 100, I get calls and emails asking how some companies, especially the new ones, broke into the Top 100. There are only two sure ways to get into the WashTech Top 100: acquire one of them or sell your company to one of them. Other than that, you'll need to work your way up the ladder. Here are a few thoughts for upward migration.

Market Commitment. GovCon is not a part time gig, and those approaching it as an adjunct to their B2B business really need to understand the differences. This is exacerbated if you're a public company, and your Board and shareholders have expectations beyond what's attainable. Public companies do succeed in this market but only when the Board, investors, and Wall Street understand that B2G is not a business based on quarterly reports.

The necessary commitment involves bringing in the right talent, dedicating the right resources, and adequately funding each. The commitment must be company-wide and the acceptance of the glacial nature of GovCon must be a given.

Focus. This can take many forms: the focus on a particular technology or agency, focus on a special problem facing those in certain jobs, a regional focus, and more. Or possibly a combination of two or more of these. Focus on what you do best, then become among the best at what you do. This is not lost on the GovCon community.

Target establishing a beachhead in an agency and grow that business before thinking about migrating to other agencies. Develop a significant presence and understand that you need to earn this position daily, not simply when you win the contract.

Time. Government time can seem like geologic ages. Things don't usually happen quickly. Those seeking rapid migration to the top tiers of contracting, to be on par with GDIT, Northrop and others, are in the wrong business unless they have deep enough pockets to buy their way in.

Time and a seriously thought-out long-term plan are required. I've several anecdotes of those who were beginning to succeed, then made an alteration to their plan which short-circuited their growth. I've other anecdotes for the flip side: companies that made alterations that were well thought out and led to winning more business.

Relationships. Those who read my articles and other posts know that I believe relationships are the key to success. These relationships include the client relationship, partner (prime/sub) relationship, management to employee, company to the channel, press relations, and more. Each must be handled properly and professionally. Snafus in any of these will impact your brand in the market as word of said snafu will invariably get out somehow (think White House leaks).

Education. This market continues to evolve, and the evolution requires perpetual education for each discipline in your company, including sales, marketing, BD, proposals, accounting, and legal. There are many venues for education, including associations, conferences, seminars, webinars, briefings, in-house training, continuing professional education, and advanced degrees (I'm an adjunct professor in the GWU graduate school for Government Contracting where I learn as much from my students as they do from me).

There is education by osmosis, hanging out with market experts (in and outside of your company), and education by the continual scanning of market information (trade publications, blogs, and other sources of market intel). But the education must be constant. Take a break for a few months and you're behind the curve.

Rinse and repeat (and re-commit). Your commitment to the market must be renewed regularly and formally or informally. This is a requirement for those seeking to move up in the pecking order, from third tier to second, from second tier to first. Of course, there are no guarantees that you will migrate to the top even if you do all these things. But I can guarantee that you will fail if you don't do them. "Do or don't, there is no try."

So, you're a new manager

This was originally published on Govloop in 2014 but could have been written in 1980 or 2020! – Mike

One of the more intimidating but significant times in the life of a marketing, BD, proposal, or line manager is the start of a new organizational assignment. It's an opportunity to take advantage of your strengths and work on any weaknesses. And, as with any project, the way you begin is extremely important.

Performing a situational assessment of your new organizational unit should be a priority. This will help you identify the major risks, challenges, and constraints to accomplishing your mission. Two effective ways to do this and to build trust are to hold an introductory meeting and to have individual get acquainted sessions.

There are differing opinions on whether to have the meeting or individual sessions first. My preference is to hold a meeting as soon as possible. Your new staff is already forming impressions and the sooner you engage, the better the chance you'll be able to manage their expectations. You might want to talk to your new supervisor and subordinate managers, if you have any, about organizational or staff sensitivities you should be aware of that might influence your plans.

Here are **ten steps** to keep in mind while you navigate your first few weeks:

1. **Focus.** Begin and end the kick-off meeting on time. Stick to an agenda and defer more lengthy discussions and digressions to another time.
2. **Introduce.** Ask each person to briefly explain his or her role in the organization (what's their job product or service).
3. **Share.** Summarize your background. Keep it short! Your team will be interested in getting to know you and might also be wondering what kind of manager you're going to be. Avoid being a windbag.
4. **Meet.** Tell each person you look forward to meeting with them individually to understand how you can help them accomplish their job and to listen to any concerns or suggestions they have. You might say that you don't believe in change just for change's sake but are interested in suggestions that will improve process and results.
5. **Listen.** Remember that people have different learning styles. And these different approaches to communication can be the dividing line between organizational unity and dysfunction. Listening is one of the things you must do to find out the things you don't already know.
6. **Be patient.** Avoid trying to solve problems – especially the institutional ones – right away. You will want to have your individual meetings and then discuss any issues with your new boss and your subordinate managers before taking any actions.
7. **Maintain.** Don't lose control of the meeting. Your group might have someone who likes to take over the discussion. If necessary, enforce a two-minute comment rule. The "talker" won't like it, but the others will love you for it! Use your facilitator skills to give everyone an opportunity to talk; you can go around the room to draw out the quiet ones.

8. **Reinforce.** You can also do a brief exercise to emphasize effective team interpersonal communication norms. Basically, brainstorm how the group would like to work together – a short list of dos and don'ts without any judgment on your part. On flip chart paper or a projected document, draw a line across the top and a line down the middle – on the left side list behaviors people like to see and on the right side list the things they don't like – either from their co-workers or you as their boss. This will help you get a better understanding of their personalities and their hot buttons. It will also give you a tool to use in the future to reinforce positive behaviors.
9. **Engage.** Everyone in your new organization deserves respect. Effective managers care about their employees. Progressive leaders don't hide in their offices, expecting everyone to visit them while they sit on their thrones. Instead, they engage in meaningful discussions with their peers and employees. The individual sessions are get-acquainted and information gathering expeditions. So, listen ten times/talk one time!
10. **Lead.** Finally, a few words about being a successful leader. Having the power and authority to make things happen isn't the same as being a leader. Set clear objectives, acquire the necessary resources, inspire your staff to care about these goals and then allow them to excel.

Don't make these three LinkedIn mistakes

I've written several articles over the years about mistakes people make on LinkedIn. – Mark

Here are just three common mistakes from a long list of LinkedIn mistakes that I've identified through observation and by reading posts from other LinkedIn trainers and experts.

The first and most glaring is having no profile picture or an inappropriate picture.

Research shows that profiles without a photo of the member are more likely to be passed over. Many LinkedIn experts argue that the photo, or headshot, is the most important feature of a profile. I'm inclined to agree, but it's only part of the puzzle.

Inappropriate photos include using actors, actresses and cartoon characters, photos in bars or at parties, and photos of boats and cars.

The standard photo should be you, in business or business casual attire, smiling, looking at the camera. Your head should be at least 50 percent of the photo.

The second mistake is not editing the headline (the line directly under your name).

The default mode is your current job title, and most job titles don't say two important things: what you bring to the table and the niche in the market you serve.

Nick Straiter of NetApp (he was at Brocade when I first met him), is a Federal Account Executive. This would show up under his name if he didn't edit that space. Instead of FAE, Nick writes: "Empowering DOE/NASA customers to solve mission critical problems with world-class enterprise data management solutions."

Nick explains what he does and who he does it for in his headline. This immediately tells the viewer if they should be reading more or moving on to the next profile.

The third mistake is omitting the summary or simply doing a resume cut and paste job.

The summary can be used in many ways, but if there is any "universal" way to start a summary, I suggest beginning with a question, or a short series of questions. These should be written to entice legitimate prospects to read more.

I start my summary with these: *"Ever ask yourself why your B2G marketing program has little or no results? Do you wonder if LinkedIn can generate more business for you? SMEs not getting attention? If you answer yes to any of the above, we should talk."*

My questions focus on three areas I specialize in: marketing to the government, LinkedIn and building a SME market position.

Supply chain logistics expert Dave Peterson starts his summary with these: *"Do you need to improve the performance of your organization's inventory investment? Are you looking for an impartial, thoroughgoing assessment of your firm's service parts management practices? Would you like to deepen your team's inventory management skillset?"*

Dave's questions focus the reader on supply chain inventory management, his area of expertise.

If questions aren't germane to the viewer of the profile, they'll move on. If they are relevant, the person viewing the profile is more likely to read more, and possibly reach out.

Each of these is "above the fold" – all visible when you open someone's profile: the headshot, the headline and the first few lines of the summary. They are immediately visible when you click on the profile, no scrolling necessary. A visit to your profile is often your "first impression" and it must be good.

Breaking up is hard to do

Good managers find ways to let go of poor employees and bad habits from Federal Computer Week in 2005. – Mike

Letting go of attachments to things that no longer have value is difficult. In the personal realm, this includes dysfunctional relationships, unhealthy habits and, in my case, the compulsive need to make bad puns. Whether you're a marketing, sales, capture, or line manager or executive, letting go takes on an even broader context because it affects not only your feelings but also your organization's success and co-workers' performance.

An effective manager realizes that allowing someone to remain in a job that doesn't fit harms that person, the other staff, and the business. Many leaders are averse to conflict and prefer to maintain a negative status quo rather than confront a performance issue directly. But problems rarely go away without some intervention. You sometimes need to let go of staff members so they can find other job opportunities better suited to their skills. Managers who were promoted from technical positions sometimes get mired in the details of a project, preferring to hide in the comfort zone of their previous responsibilities.

Managers who won't delegate tasks can cripple an organization. If you can't delegate, you will demoralize your employees and stall your career. While you remain buried in minutiae, important management decisions go unattended. Letting go of less important technical details takes courage but is a sign of a mature manager. People also get emotionally invested in certain design approaches, management solutions, technology projects and, in the case of industry, specific government business opportunities.

It can be difficult to separate enthusiasm, a positive trait, from an inability or unwillingness to objectively evaluate alternatives. If you're not careful, you can waste money on a losing proposition because You're unwilling to recognize a flawed plan.

When deciding whether to proceed with a plan or not, I like to use a decision matrix that requires the major stakeholders to assess the viability of an idea or project by scoring each critical success factor. If used properly, this approach can remove the raw emotions from the equation. What's left is an objective view of whether the return on investment justifies the costs of workforce, IT infrastructure and financial resources.

People often avoid letting go because they fear uncertainty. But the act of moving on creates possibilities for something better. On the other side of uncertainty lies tremendous business and personal potential.

Enlightened managers aren't afraid to take calculated risks. They accept that the status quo is not a friend to be trusted for too long. As the song goes, "breaking up is hard to do." But if you do, a new world of opportunities awaits you.

Amtower's rules of speaker engagement

Here are several lessons learned from doing many coveted GovCon speaking gigs. – Mark

We've all been part of the audience when the speaker:

- Thinks way too much of himself and wants to tell you that you should, too.
- Is so boring, you long for the professor who put you to sleep.
- Has a monotone that causes a downturn in the economy.

If you want to get on the podium (virtual or otherwise), don't be one of those people.

Speaking engagements in our market seem to be available frequently, but only a very small percentage of those in GovCon will get the opportunity to present at industry events.

Why? First, many speaking slots are tied directly to a sponsorship of the event. Others require filling out the necessary forms even to be considered. Usually this is some sort of "call for papers," where the event web site will have a tab that asks for potential speakers to suggest a germane topic, then fill out the required paperwork to be considered. Hint: Monitor association sites for upcoming conferences and look for those "call for paper" announcements. At AFCEA, one way the Small Business Committee identifies speakers and topics is to ask members to recommend suggest names for the events committee. Some event producers will invite the known SMEs when their topics are part of the program.

I've been extremely fortunate over the years to get many GovCon speaking gigs, and many of those are return engagements for annual events.

Why me? To get the full answer you'd have to ask the event producers, but in part it involves my ability to stay within the parameters of what that producer wants. If it's a moderating role, I moderate, not act as a panelist. If I have a fifteen-minute window to speak, I stay within the time limit. And I always try to stick to the assigned topic.

I also work hard to get selected to speak. If you also want to get speaking gigs in this market, here are some things to consider:

- First and foremost, know your subject matter inside out. Be prepared for questions both related to your topic and tangential to the topic. If you don't know the answer, don't fake it. Tell the person you will do research and get back to them.
- Rehearse your presentation out loud to yourself. If you have slides, go through them several times to get your timing and segues down. Join a local Toastmasters to improve.
- Do NOT read your slides verbatim. We've all had to sit through those presentations, and they are simply boring. If you use notes, refer to them but don't read them.
- No cheap shots or off-color humor. Audience sensitivities vary widely so it's best to play it safe and avoid areas of controversy. Along those same lines totally avoid politics or religion.

- Always add value. I often hear back from producers, audience surveys, and attendees that I gave them things they could act upon that day.
- As I mentioned above, stay within your time allotment. I've been slotted behind people who go over their time by as much as 15-20 minutes -- a couple of times even longer. There is a schedule, and you have a slot. So, stay within that time slot.
- If it's a public event, help with the promotion. Post it in LinkedIn and Facebook, tweet it, and send it your email distribution. I include my speaking gigs as part of my email signature, and I invite people individually.
- Show enthusiasm for your topic. Have a point of view and let it come out when you're on stage. People don't want to hear the same platitudes over and over. They want something that causes them to think or act.
- Do NOT pitch from the podium – this is not the time of place to sell yourself or your company. You may mention what you do once if it's germane. Once is plenty. Twice is annoying.
- Know who the audience is. Address their concerns and respect them. They are giving their time to you, and they deserve your best effort.
- Never act disappointed if the audience is not as big as you hoped. I've been invited to speak only to find the audience is only five people. In that instance I turned it around and made it more of a group conversation rather than a presentation and we all got more out of it. Offering something of value to even one person is a plus!

These tips should help you if you want one of the coveted speaking gigs and the exposure that comes with it.

What to ask sales job candidates

As a former BD executive, I developed these questions in the '90s. - Mike

From the number of inquiries I receive, there is an ever-increasing demand for qualified government contractor business developers. Unfortunately, predicting which candidate will succeed at your company is extremely difficult. Here are eight interview questions that might help.

1. Describe a standard business development process including the key roles.
2. Give a specific example of how you successfully identified, qualified, and then supported a bid through contract award.
3. What's the key information you need to gather to develop a viable, qualified opportunity?
4. Which government agencies have you had success selling to?
5. How much time do you spend at your desk versus meeting with prospects and teaming partners? (Adjust this as necessary to consider remote working.)
6. How would you spend your first 90 days in your new job?
7. What factors do you believe should drive a bid versus no bid decision?
8. What's the optimal way for business development to work with operations?

Even if you find someone who nails all eight questions, there is still the matter of what your intuition is telling you about the person and, of course, whether your company has the BD focus, process, and resources necessary to enable BD success. But that's a topic for another time.

Small business contractors' new year to-do's

I wrote this article at the end of 2021 in the middle of the pandemic hoping that small businesses would adequately prepare for the new year. – Mark

Come Jan. '21, there will be a new administration, changing missions and new priorities. Some departments and agencies will be looking down the road to a larger budget and new programs, some departments and agencies will see less.

Arguably larger contractors will have an easier time shifting resources to address the new directions, but all contractors will be impacted by the transition.

Small and small mid-size contractors will have a more difficult time regardless of where their client agency falls in the mix. If their client agency is on the receiving end of a larger budget, there will likely be more competition. If their client is going to get less, there will be fewer contract dollars to go around.

So, what should the small and smaller mid-tier contractors do?

My recommendation for smaller contractors is to start by beefing up your client relationships: build deeper and stronger connections in the agencies where you currently have the most work.

Account-based marketing (ABM) is a new buzzword in B2B marketing, but we have successfully employed it in GovCon for decades.

Regardless of where the fiscal 2022 budget goes, there will still be spending across the board, but you need to put yourself in a position to maximize your presence in the agencies where you do business.

So how can you build deeper relationships in your core agencies? There are several ways, including:

- Have on-site staff gather intel through conversations with those they work with.
- Monitor the trade media for any references of your target agencies and look up the people quoted on LinkedIn. Post the article and tag the quoted personnel. You're now on their radar.
- Monitor the virtual events where your target agencies will have speakers and attend.
- Look up the agencies on LinkedIn. All federal departments, agencies and major operating divisions have company pages on LinkedIn. Search for their personnel and sort by job title. Start reaching out.
- And don't forget the traditional method of reaching out: pick up the phone and call current customers to determine what they think about how the new priorities will impact their programs.

Even when the pandemic restrictions start to loosen up, many of our new habits will be partially ingrained: more virtual (Zoom) meetings and strategically leveraging LinkedIn.

I wish you the best of luck as we move into the new year!

The power of old-fashioned conversations

This article published Washington Technology in 2015 based on a transformative experience I had in 1998. – Mike

I appreciate the ability to share vital information and coordinate activities using email, texts, LinkedIn and Facebook. But, because of some previous challenging interpersonal relationships, I have also learned that when it comes to the lively world of human emotions, blogger beware!

Buddhist scholar Daisaku Ikeda has said, *"We live in the midst of a flood of soulless information. And the more we rely on one-way communication...the more I feel the need to stress the value of the sound of the human voice. The simple but precious interaction of voice and voice, person and person, the exchange of life with life."*

There was a time in the 1990s, when no matter how hard I tried, I couldn't get along with one of my work colleagues, "Bob." He was an operations VP, and I was the business development VP. Bob had a way of getting under everyone's skin -- especially through the tone of his emails. My responses, which seemed so innocent and compassionate at the time, only made him more antagonistic.

I reflected a lot about this relationship and received encouragement from an advisor to close my eyes and imagine that I was someone whose compassion I greatly respected talking to my coworker. Instead of firing off a quick email response to yet another angry message that had landed in my inbox, I visualized Ikeda walking from my office down to Bob's and, using a very warm voice, asking him how he was doing. I realized then that this was the caring attitude I needed to manifest to help bring out Bob's own compassion.

The very next day, Bob and I ended up waiting for a government official in a conference room. I asked him how his family was doing. He said his teenage daughter had been diagnosed with diabetes a year before and had been refusing to take her insulin treatments. This was causing their family a lot of stress. I mentioned to him that it was also a very difficult time for me because Most Beautiful One, my wife of 52 years, had recently been diagnosed with multiple sclerosis. With this heart-to-heart sharing, Bob and I went from a relationship built on distrust to one of mutual respect. I have never forgotten this experience.

According to researchers, about 7 percent of our communications is what we say, 38 percent is the way we say it - rate, tone, and inflection - and 55 percent is our body language before, during and after we say it.

So, what we write to one another needs to be extremely concise to be correctly understood. E-mail, texts, and social media posts are missing the crucial sounds of a human voice and the visual context clues that let us know what the sender is feeling and if the recipient is greatly upset, mildly peeved, or encouraged.

It often takes person-to-person dialogue to understand someone else's true intention and to improve a negative situation. It is one of the ways I try to create harmony in my surroundings.

When I feel compelled to write an emotional e-mail or text, I send it to myself and reread it the next day before forwarding it to others. By taking time to reflect, I can ask myself why I don't just call or Zoom with the source of my frustration rather than slinging a one-sided written message. Such barbs are impossible to recall and can cause considerable damage. How do I know if the recipient really understood what I meant if I can't see or at least talk to that person?

It takes our collective wisdom to use the full spectrum of human communication channels to build healthy relationships, communities, and organizations. So, the next time I have the urge to send some angry written words off into the World Wide Web, I will make a phone call instead.

Why don't some small businesses win more?

It's important for small businesses to understand the investment required to enter the GOVCON market. – Mark

Several years ago, American Express OPEN commissioned studies on what it takes for small contractors to succeed in GovCon. Two of the salient issues from these studies that still apply today are these:

- It takes a significant investment of time and money to learn about the market. The first study indicated an average of $87,000/year to get started successfully. This included leveraging both internal and external resources. The second study, about three years later, moved the financial needle up to $120,000 a year.
- The average time to winning business was about 20 months, better than a year and a half. The timeframe was the same in both studies.

While there were several other factors involved, the studies basically showed how much groundwork needed to be laid prior to even going after contracts. This verified what many of us advising small contractors had been saying for years.

While the American Express study was done for those just starting out in government contracting, some of the issues are the same for many contractors that have won already some business but are having a hard time reaching any sort of critical mass.

Many smaller companies still don't grasp that winning government business requires expertise in several areas, and if you don't have those skills internally, you need to leverage outside resources to win business and grow, resources both in people and information resources.

Having worked with many small government contractors over the last 35 years, I've made note of several areas where small contractors need help. Many small business owners tend to underestimate the value of several professional positions: accounting, HR, legal, business development, marketing, and someone to respond to bids. Many of those same business owners overestimate their own talent in those areas.

Accounting. This is not my area, but I've seen many companies lose business because of not being compliant in this area. Unless your accountant has sufficient experience in government contracting, you need to get a specialist. Many of the back-office functions (accounting, HR, etc.) can be outsourced to companies like Cordia or Insperity.

Legal. Again, not my arena, but the laws and regulations pertaining to government contracting are complex and require someone with deep expertise. Steve Koprince's book, *The Small Business Guide to Government Contracts,* remains the best source to start learning about the issues. There are several legal firms, like Offit Kurman, that help small contractors.

Bid Tracking. Then there is the reliable marketing data issue: being unwilling to obtain outside resources for bid tracking, services like BGov (Bloomberg Government). Many small contractor executives believe (or hope) that following FedBizOps (www.fbo.gov) will be sufficient, thinking anything within their NAICS is within their scope. They ignore or fail to grasp that by the time the bid shows up on FBO, many others are already far down the road of teaming to bid, influencing the SOW, and more. More robust bid platforms will help you find opportunities that match your capabilities earlier in the cycle.

To further complicate the problem, too many small contractors don't attend educational and networking forums, places where they could pick up tips or meet others with whom they might team. Some have experimented with networking venues and simply attended the wrong one, then concluded they were all a waste of time. Finding the right venues for networking and education are key for a small business to grow.

The same holds true for picking the right association to join. Selecting the wrong one can leave a bad taste. For example, AFCEA has a great small contractor program, but if you don't know about it or don't take the time to attend, it doesn't do much good. The local chamber may have a "GovCon" committee, but it will most likely lack the resources to be truly helpful.

It seems that many small contractors (especially those unwilling to pay for outside expertise) still rely on burning incense and chanting to the FBO, OSDBU and SBA deities to deliver them the path to winning contracts. If they remain unwilling to vet and select good outside sources, they will be short timers in GovCon.

Find the right lead tracking system

Having been in the GovCon world since the 1970s, I've developed some strong opinions about tracking sales leads. – Mike

When it comes to lead tracking systems, there is no "one size fits all" solution. I've successfully implemented Salesforce, spreadsheets, complex databases, etc. and I've learned the hard way that organizations shouldn't implement anything they don't have the resources to maintain. Better to track five to ten fields per opportunity that can be kept current by BD and capture staff than 30 fields that are always out of date.

Every commercial off the shelf solution will require some degree of modification to fit your business development (BD) process and reporting requirements. From a management perspective, the lead tracking system reporting capabilities are as important as the ability to collect opportunity information.

Find a tool that enables a capture team to analytically assess the readiness to bid and win probability for an opportunity and then shows the relative management/technical and price health (green, yellow, red) for all the opportunities in the pipeline.

Regardless of the tool, some kind of lead tracking system is essential to bring discipline and focus to new business capture and bid decision activities. The alternative is BD crisis management.

Speaking of new business pipelines -- they can look so impressive with all the sales leads in their neat rows. But, if you dig below the surface, you'll discover you can't always believe what you read. Here are ten indicators I look for to determine if the content of a lead tracking system is worth the paper it's printed on.

- There aren't enough higher win probability opportunities to generate the desired orders and revenue.
- Senior management has decreed that the pipeline will be filled without taking a serious look at the whether there are sufficient BD, capture, and proposal resources and whether the organization is adhering to an effective BD process.
- As a result of a lack of oversight or the previous bullet, too many opportunities in the pipeline are outside the company's current capabilities, target clients or target services.
- The status of several opportunities hasn't been updated for months.
- Opportunities aren't progressing through the standard BD phases (qualification, capture, proposal). Or, if they are, too few low probability bids are being dropped early enough.
- Win probability estimates are too subjective, lacking analytical justification.
- The pipeline has too many unqualified leads with near term RFPs that should be dropped.
- Projected RFP, contract award and contract start-up dates are too optimistic.
- There aren't regularly scheduled weekly or bi-weekly pipeline status reviews.

- Line (operations or engineering) management hasn't bought off on the opportunities that market research or BD has entered into the pipeline. Great opportunities are useless if no one is working them.

It's not an uncommon phenomenon in the contracting community, commercial or government, for companies to have to cut back spending in the late summer or fall. The later you wait to adjust the budget, the more drastic the corrections will be including having to let go critical indirect staff. Of course, this implies knowing how real your sales pipeline is and how accurate the RFP projections. Establish budgets according to more conservative revenue estimates as opposed to aggressive projections. This change needs to start at the top with the CEO, VP of Sales & Marketing, and CFO.

A new business pipeline is only as useful as the quality of its opportunities and the company's ability to refine them as additional information is gathered. Otherwise, garbage in will definitely result in garbage out.

Leveraging marketing resources is critical

For over three decades, I've been encouraging small businesses to embrace marketing to experience business success. – Mark

Small contractors need to think seriously about marketing, about how to integrate it into the corporate culture and use customer touch points and social activity as opportunities to market the company, to tell their story in ways that resonate with the niche they serve. They operate at a perpetual resource disadvantage, so defining and leveraging the resources that are available should be job one. And that applies to marketing as much or more than any other function.

Why? Larger contractors often have entire departments dedicated to marketing the company by getting their subject matter experts speaking gigs, sponsoring various industry events, getting stories in trade media -- basically dominating much of the traditional marketing landscape.

One primary objective of the Government Contractor Survey released by Market Connections was to identify best practices of winning government contractors, including small contractors. Some solutions to the issues the study points out don't require cash outlays, but instead require a well-constructed game plan of what's "do-able".

Three specific findings for small contractors are creating a thought leadership/subject matter position, differentiating beyond price, and content marketing. Each of these is well within the reach of companies of any size.

Thought Leadership/Subject Matter (TL/SME) Expertise. This was the top item of importance in the Market Connections study and has been on the rise for several years. Regardless of size, if a company has expertise in a specific area, they can and should present it in multiple ways to the community they serve. Building a thought leader/subject matter expert market position takes time and a demonstrable area of expertise. This is first demonstrated in the work you perform.

Other elements of the TL/SME platform include a deep, current knowledge of a specialized subject, the ability to explain the complex in easily understood terms, sharing the knowledge in multiple venues (thought leaders don't operate in a vacuum. They need to be seen and heard). They also need to know what influences are occurring in their niche and how those influences might impact the future of this specialty. Clearly, thought leadership is not for the timid or lazy.

Differentiating Beyond Price. Differentiation is a major step in developing any competitive advantage over the competition, and needs to be a goal, especially for small contractors. It's also a major component of a thought leadership platform.

The process of differentiation starts with identifying your area of expertise, then looking for ways to show how the company is different, and then explaining why this is important to the buying audience. Take Health IT as an example. Many companies have built up Health IT practices. Overlay that with data analytics, another hot topic in our market. You have combined two significant factors.

Want to differentiate further? In the Health business, especially at CMS and SSA, there is a fair amount of fraud. So, now you can highlight four differentiators: health IT and data analytics, further differentiated by having FWA expertise (fraud, waste, and abuse). Finally, overlay this with a specific agency, like CMS. There are many ways to differentiate your area of expertise, assuming you have one.

Content Marketing. A study from Forrester Research shows that 57 percent of the buying decision is made before vendor outreach. Admittedly this is B2B, not B2G, but the same premise applies in B2G.

Studies by Market Connections demonstrate the power of content throughout the procurement process. Producing and sharing content that educates the buyer while highlighting a company's area of expertise puts them on the radar and gives the buyer a sense of comfort regarding their skill level.

Generating good content doesn't require huge cash outlays. It requires having something important to say, and a venue to share. Blogs are easy to launch and to populate with content germane to your audience. With a blog you can start slowly and build some momentum. And, like differentiation, content is critical to developing a thought leader/subject matter expert market position.

Creating market share and developing a plan for growth is an incremental process. For a small contractor, integrating marketing into the company culture is a core issue for survival and growth. Leveraging the tools and tactics that incur minimal or no cost is critical.

How to assess customer influence

The importance of understanding who in an agency will influence a procurement led to this article. – Mike

During the procurement process, there may be several people and/or organizations that can influence the award. The most obvious is the individual or organization within the Customer group that will receive the proposed products/services. Others, such as your company superiors, peers, and supporting organizations, also can affect the award.

In many cases, different people will have different views on their Understanding of the Problem; they may also have different views on key requirements, the Evaluation Criteria, and the components of a successful solution.

This is an example of a chart you can use in the capture plan to illustrate these key individuals and your estimate of their degree of involvement in the selection process.

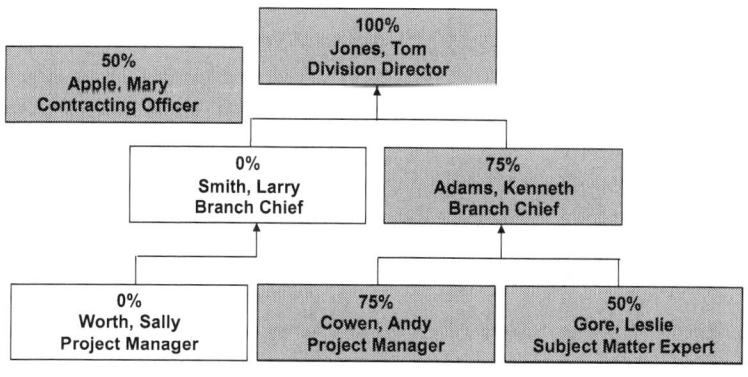

% = Probability of Involvement

The purpose of positioning activities is to positively influence the customer prior to the release of the request for proposal.

Actions should be taken to:

- Establish strong relationships with all key customer decision makers and influencers.
- Demonstrate technical insight.
- Get the PM & technical experts wanted by the customer.
- Form the right team of subcontractors.
- Develop and communicate a creative, workable solution to the customer's problems.
- Influence the SOW with your company's discriminators through white papers, contacts, etc.

Don't be a Waldo – stand out

I'm always trying to find analogies to help my clients improve their marketing. – Mark

Anybody know Martin Handford? Probably doesn't ring a bell, right?

How about *Where's Waldo*? Does that ring your doorbell? Handford produced/drew the popular book series starting in 1987. I've a few in my library. My daughter could always find Waldo before me. So could my wife and son… hell, probably the cat, too.

Great, Mark. What's the point? Even though Waldo dresses differently, when he is in a crowd he doesn't really stand out. Why? Because he's in a crowd. If you're a small IT services firm in the government market, you have the same problem: Standing out from the crowd.

Over the years I've had numerous discussions with Offices of Small, Disadvantaged Business Utilization, Small Business Liaison Offices, program managers and senior business development personnel in large contractors about the best ways for small companies to approach agencies and primes in that first face-to-face meeting. There are several themes that come up in virtually every conversation. Here they are, in no particular order. For our purposes, our small contractor will be a fictitious company, TSSIE (pronounced tiz-zee: The Smallest Systems Integrator Ever).

- **They (TSSIE) don't know us.** TSSIE comes in having done little or no research about the agency or prime contractor. They don't know what the agency or contractor needs and/or they are unfamiliar with the scope of the contracts involved. They are, however, prepared to talk about themselves.
- **They lead with a non-starter.** TSSIE leads with their set-aside status. OSDBUs, SBLOs and program managers don't care about your status. They care about your *skills*. What are you really good at and do I need it for my agency or my team?
- **They are an IT generalist.** TSSIE claims expertise in 10 or more IT specialties, yet only has 5 employees. TSSIE's response to each question is "Yeah, we can do that."
- **They tout a non-strength**. TSSIE brags to primes that 60 percent of its employees have security clearances (3 of the 5 employees). Prime responds by saying that only 4 percent of its workforce (4,700 out of 117,500) are cleared.

So how should TSSIE present itself as a differentiated contractor in a face-to-face meeting? TSSIE should:

- Present itself as a knowledgeable contractor. Always do research before a meeting.
- Small companies cannot be expert in several things, so pick a niche you're good at and work hard at becoming better.
- Small companies need to focus on just one or two agencies and get to know them well. Develop relationships with key staff inside the client agency.
- Whether it's an agency or prime, look them up on LinkedIn before the meeting to learn more about the people you'll meet.

- When getting ready for an OSDBU/SBLO visit, read the OMB 53 submission, scour the agency web site, search the trade media for any agency information, especially about contract preferences.
- If asked about a peripheral area, indicate whether you have done it before, but be honest and say it's not a strength if it isn't.
- If you have good CPARS and good client relationships, say so. Both past performance and knowing the players are key to progressing.
- Develop a list of questions pertinent to the meeting, things that came up during your research. You can use rhetorical questions to support or refute some of your assumptions.
- Take detailed notes, or if possible, bring someone just to take notes.
- Have a one-pager (not a dossier) on your capabilities and current contracts. Include both NAICS and PSCs. Also, SINs if they are specific, like CDM. If you have a set-aside status, list it.

One of the services I offer my clients is strategic introductions, but I don't make the intro if the client is not prepared. You may only get one chance for a face-to-face meeting, so you need to make the most of it.

So, what's the *Waldo* connection? If you don't stand out in that first face-to-face meeting, you're doomed to become just another face in the crowd, only no one will be looking for you.

Must-have bid pursuit and decision processes

I first wrote about the opportunity pursuit and bid decision processes in the 1990s. This is an updated version of this original article. – Mike

The time and money so many government contractors and sales professionals waste qualifying and chasing new business opportunities could, with a little honest introspection, be eliminated. That's why I encourage my clients to employ a pursuit decision-making process - a simple matrix comprised of a set of key questions that, if not answered in the affirmative, result in the decision not to continue. The use of such a decision tool also tends to objectify decisions -- taking unnecessary emotions out of the equation.

Here is an example of a typical set of WHETHER TO PURSUE (pursuit) decision questions from one small government contractor's matrix that help avoid wasting valuable resources chasing poor opportunities:

1. Is a significant part of this work consistent with one of our four core competencies?
2. Will we be perceived as a credible prime contractor? Or, if a sub, will a prime need our competencies or experience with this client to win?
3. Is it in a target location and/or with a target client?
4. If there is a major incumbent, are they vulnerable and are we (our team) potentially strong/big enough to unseat them?
5. Is there a reasonable chance of it being a funded project?
6. If a very small task (< $250K), is it of strategic importance (also see #1 above)? Could it result in more substantial business?

7. Is there enough time to adequately market the client prior to an RFP being released?

Try it – with a little discipline, the return on investment is impressive and inspiring!

I also strongly recommend institutionalizing a WHETHER TO BID decision process. Here are eleven indispensable criteria that no respectable contractor should be without! These can easily be presented in a table format with numerical or color scoring.

1. Is this bid consistent with your strategic focus (competencies, target markets, staffing location & labor costs)?
2. What's your overall ability to meet the technical requirements (Discriminators)?
3. Do you have the past performance necessary to win the job?
4. Do you have the available key personnel including a Project Manager?
5. How much risk is there to successfully executing this contract (Do you really want to win)?
6. Have you marketed the client and established a good rapport and credibility?
7. Will this contract be profitable?
8. Can you be sufficiently cost competitive?
9. How much competition is there?
10. Do you have the necessary available proposal resources and the time to do a good proposal?
11. Are you viewed as a credible prime contractor or, if subcontracting, is your prime considered credible?

Each company will have its own take on these factors. But the answers to some version of these questions will either convince you of the folly of pursuing and then submitting a proposal or help identify weaknesses that need to be remedied for you to win.

There are two common approaches to bid/no bid decision-making. The first one (see figure) is authoritarian.

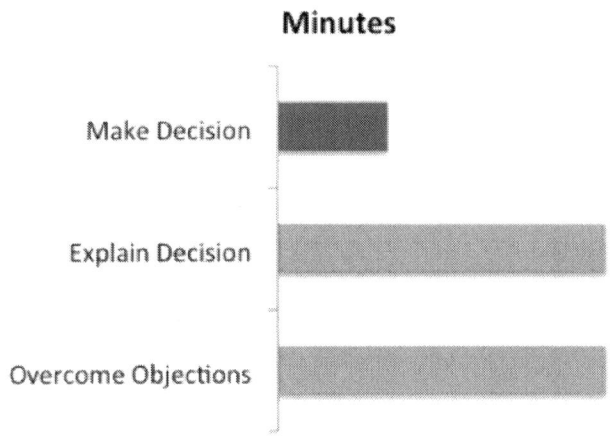

The manager makes the decision based on the knowledge she can gather. Let's say this takes ten minutes. Then it will probably take her 30 minutes to explain the decision to the group and another 30 minutes to gain their acceptance by overcoming their objections.

The alternative (see the figure on next page) is to have a group who share ideas and analyses and agree on the final bid decision.

Studies show that the group often has values, feelings, and reactions quite different from those the manager supposes they have. And no one knows these preferences and experiences as well as the group itself.

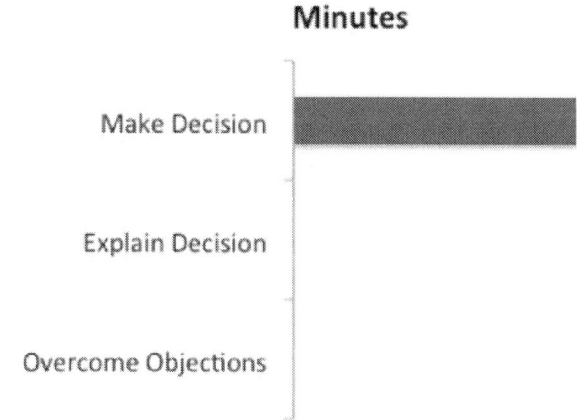

Organizations that embrace group decision making on more important matters, like whether to pursue a strategic bid or not, typically have a higher success rate and don't have to spend nearly as much time explaining and convincing. It takes at least twice as much time to follow the tired old authoritarian approach.

However, it's also important for the organization to recognize that there is a time for groupthink and time for decisive action. In other words, sometimes you just have to make the decision. To know the difference is one of the most critical roles of a leader.

In general, there are usually four possible outcomes of a bid decision meeting:

1. **No bid**. The first, and for many companies the most difficult, is to say no to the bid. I've had clients tell me one of my major contributions was to help them say no. There are many reasons for this reluctance to kill a bid including a fear of going against a strong individual's attachment to the bid, not wanting to have to admit that any investment up to this point was wasted, an unfounded confidence in your competitiveness, and pressure to fill the new business pipeline. In other words, to make the numbers look good.
2. **Delay decision.** I know some leaders whose response to a fear of making the wrong decision, is to delay it. This can be especially frustrating to a proposal team that is waiting to start a proposal as they watch the proposal due date rapidly approaching. It's even more damaging when it occurs after RFP release. Maybe someone should pass a law that all executives must work on at least one proposal, so they understand the impact their bid decisions have on the staff they rely on to do the work. However, delaying a decision can provide time for additional thoughtful and extended analysis and new alternatives to be recognized or created. For instance, with further meetings with other companies and the customer, you may decide not to prime one job but to subcontract another.
3. **Contingent bid.** Sometimes a bid decision is contingent on some condition being met. For instance, the identification of a project manager or key teammate to include in the proposal, resolution with the government contracting officer of a potential conflict of interest, or the determination as to whether the client has a favored contractor, and it isn't you!
4. **Bid.** The final possible outcome is to decide to bid. And, of course, then the real fun begins!

Making an informed bid decision is perhaps the weakest link for most government contractors. Too many decisions are based on emotions, insufficient marketing intelligence and a lack of discussion. This results in wasted resources and a lower win bid rate. Here are some of the major reasons a no bid decision should be considered:

- Bid and proposal funds aren't available to pursue the bid
- Key teammates aren't available
- The product or solution doesn't meet the client's requirements
- Required capabilities or skills are absent
- Your company is too late in the game
- Key client relationships have not been established
- Your competitive position is weak
- You have a limited knowledge of the procurement
- Required key personnel candidates have not been identified
- Your proposal resources are insufficient
- A strongly positioned low-cost bidder emerges
- The contract terms & conditions in the request for proposal or quote are unacceptable

In my experience, it takes several No's to leave room for a Yes.

Five steps to stand out from the crowd

My clients often come to me for help in these five areas. – Mark

It's Friday afternoon and I get a call from a friend asking for a brief overview of fiscal 2018 IT spending. They need it ASAP for a presentation the following week. I email two friends at BGov, and they get back to me within an hour with five perfect slides.

I send it to my friend, and everyone is happy. Then I start looking at the slides a little more closely. And I think about the money going out to IT, and how it's going to be spent. And I think about the smaller companies I'm working with and those I want to work with.

What should they do to win some of this money? How can they stand out from the crowd to get some of those precious government contract dollars? Several things come to mind but these five are usually at the top of my list.

1. **Networking**. We all understand that this market is driven by relationships: who you know, who knows you, what they think of you and you of them, and what you might be able to do together or for one another. In the summer of 2012, I wrote an article about networking, which is a big part of the relationship puzzle. Where you choose to spend your time is critical and there are always too many venues where you can network. Picking the events which yield the best return on investment, where you can meet prospects, customers, partners, the media, and others, is a key component to help you stand out where it matters. You must be seen to be known.

2. **Strategy**. I've been in numerous meetings where an executive has goals, sometimes nebulous, sometimes well-defined, but they lack a strategy for reaching the goals. Knowing your goals is important, but without a game plan you will likely go nowhere, and you will certainly not stand out. Mike wrote an excellent chapter earlier in this book about a streamlined strategic planning approach.
3. **Differentiate**. Clearly enunciate what you bring to the table. This can be several things that make you and your company unique, or it can be one particularly strong area of competence. Combinations can include technical expertise, deep relationships with an agency, SMEs, owning a place on preferred contracts, and set-aside status. The more you can differentiate in terms that appeal to government buyers the more you stand out.
4. **Agency (account) based marketing (ABM)**. I wrote about this in an earlier chapter, but it's worth repeating. Since the mid-1990s, I've been advising companies to maximize their presence in agencies where they are known before they try to migrate to "greener pastures," which are often agencies where they aren't know. If you're already supporting one or two existing Cabinet department level divisions, why not expand to other divisions within that department? This is often a saner approach than migrating to another cabinet department or independent agency. It's much easier to stand out when you're doing more business with your best customer(s). It's also lower risk with a higher return on sales investment.
5. **Social selling**. Social selling is an adjunct to traditional selling, leveraging social networking platforms to start and manage relationships with customers, prospects, partners, and others. Social selling is the process of finding buyers and influencers on a social networking platform (by now

you no doubt know I prefer LinkedIn), getting on their radar and sharing information that will make you and your company stand out from the competition. LinkedIn is pervasive in the government contracting community and by adding valuable insights on social media you will most definitely stand out.

Critical elements of a winning proposal

I first documented proposal development best practices in my own and then my client's BD Guides as well as in my 2010 book about winning government business — Mike

There are many factors that contribute to a winning proposal. And even though the following elements are critical (and should be non-negotiable), it is amazing how many companies fail to understand their importance. Proposals should be:

- Compliant with and traceable to every RFP requirement
- Responsive to the customer's needs and concerns
- Understandable by the average reader (not just agency subject matter experts)
- Credible -- based on substantiated claims
- Tell a story (as opposed to a disjointed treatise written by several people)
- Supported by professional graphics (minimize too many text-only pages)
- Consistent among management, technical and pricing volumes
- Carefully edited (in the client's mind, this often reflects the quality of future deliverables)

Too many companies begin proposal writing without first having a solid kick-off meeting. Depending on the complexity and type of proposal, here are some important meeting topics:

- Key procurement details and marketing intelligence
- Competition strengths and weaknesses
- Your company strengths and weaknesses

- Major themes and discriminators
- Win strategy (technical, management and price)
- Unexpected changes in the actual solicitation
- Solicitation clarifications to submit to the client
- Proposal milestone schedule including price reviews
- Teaming partner roles and responsibilities
- Writing assignments
- Writing guidelines
- Key personnel and past performance citations
- Staffing plan (if relevant)
- Proposal delivery requirements
- Actions items

One of the most useful items in a proposal manager's arsenal is boilerplate material. Boilerplate is text and graphics already created for previous proposals, marketing documents, standard project descriptions, resumes and miscellaneous publications. It can save considerable money and labor.

Project managers should be required to write a contract summary and update it at least once a year. Staff members should have a current resume. Some companies make the annual resume update an annual review requirement.

Unfortunately, most companies struggle to collect and maintain this type of information. It's one those tasks that is either not funded or too low on the priority list to get implemented. So, unless proposal writers can dig up previous proposal sections, each proposal must be written from scratch. This is both costly and frustrating.

Boilerplate material should be gathered in a shared drive or database utilizing some sort of file structure or indexing scheme that allow proposal writers to easily find it. It should also be searchable.

But even if the information is available, some contractors make the mistake of inserting boilerplate text and graphics into a proposal without carefully adapting them to the specific request for proposal requirements. The use of unmodified boilerplate can easily become habit forming. But, to government evaluators, generic proposals are also an obvious sign of laziness or a lack of competency. While it makes it easier to write the proposal, it also makes it easier to lose!

My friend Don, not Donald's real name, ran the proposal center for a large aerospace division at a west coast submarine base. He was having a very difficult time identifying project managers and engineers who understand the difference between technical writing and proposal writing. So, Don and his staff often had to work long hours re-writing or condensing proposal input. He was so frustrated that he included his resume when he emailed me with this horror story.

I emailed Don some suggestions for how he might improve his situation. These included giving writers a detailed proposal outline that describes all the requirements in each section, where graphics or tables would demonstrate the company's technical approach and individual section page limits. Companies that submit superior technical proposals have invested in proposal training for targeted line staff, made supporting a proposal part of career progression and implemented an incentive or bonus plan for proposal team members.

In my experience, when companies train people in the proposal process (through workshops and on the job), about one third take to it like a duck to water, one third just barely stay afloat and one third sink to the bottom. It's just the nature of the beast. Technical writers not only need an in-depth understanding of the technical approach – they need to be able to write concise proposal text within page constraints. Proposals, in most cases, shouldn't be written to a college level. They should be comprehensible to the average non-expert government reviewer.

The people who do make the transition to proposal writing will only succeed if their senior management enforces a consistent proposal development and bid decision process (including saying no to dumb bids) and resources. Otherwise, these wonderfully trained proposal writers will just end up frustrated.

There also must be a commitment to provide the sound infrastructure necessary to development winning proposals. This includes:

- Maintain an online proposal, resume and past performance library.
- Have a well-thought out proposal process with trained personnel.
- Develop storyboards for more complex proposals.

Themes and discriminators. Themes make inferior approaches obvious, drive us to more superior approaches, and force us to relate features to benefits. The most effective themes are:

- Substantiated sales message, point of emphasis, advantage, unique or superior benefit or supported discriminator
- Artfully woven throughout the proposal, transmittal letter, and cover graphic to unify and focus the message throughout the proposal
- Direct; they address program issues or customer concerns and are supportable with concrete evidence
- A tool to demonstrate your strengths and the competition's weaknesses (known as ghosting your competitors)
- Resonate with the proposal instructions (RFP section L) and proposal evaluation criteria (RFP section M)

The best themes can and. where possible, should also become your discriminator(s). These are:

- Non-trivial in the customer's eyes
- Unique to the company or team
- Believable and easily defendable
- Something the competition doesn't possess
- Clearly identified and substantiated in the proposal
- MUST BE ABLE TO BE SUBSTANTIATED or the evaluators will roll their eyes and give you a lower score.

Some typical top-level themes are:

- Low risk
- Our company can save you money
- Our company can save you time
- Our company can increase system performance
- Best value
- Technical excellence
- Technology application
- Innovation

- Ability to integrate all program/project functions
- Accurate reporting
- Reliable performance data
- Superior past performance
- Customer understanding
- End-user knowledge
- Program insight
- System infrastructure insight
- Effective change management
- Quality
- Corporate commitment
- Cost savings
- Communication and collaboration
- Ethical conduct
- Environmental stewardship
- Excellent safety record
- Fiscal stewardship
- Business process engineering
- Done this for you before or for someone else
- Detailed understanding of elements of success required to meet all major milestones
- Disciplined step by step processes
- Low risk approach
- Customer confidence in our people
- Time saved or money on similar programs
- Evidence of continued improvement

Some examples of technical themes are:

- How well our company understands the requirements
- What our company proposes to do – our innovative approach is based on (insert unique methodology or toolset)
- How our company proposes to do it

- Disciplined, step-by-step processes (illustrate them)
- Application of technology and automated tools
- Specialized software
- Broad experience with hardware and software (prove it)
- Quality assurance methodology

Some examples of management themes are:

- Corporate commitment
- Organizational design and rationale including client interface
- Top level project visibility
- Access to top management
- Reduced customer oversight
- Partnership
- Organizational efficiency (span of control, task management and role of teammates)
- Project team qualifications
- Prime contractor management and subcontractor management performance
- The project manager
- Key managers
- Financial control methods and track record
- Management experience with similar scope of work

Some examples of personnel themes are:

- Collective qualifications and total years of experience
- Multi-disciplinary team capable of executing and managing the program holistically
- Quantified specialized skill/experience
- Total size of team employee work force that can be applied to this contract
- Project manager and key people to be made available

- Individual commitment
- Recruiting capabilities
- Retention rates
- Bench strength
- Breadth and depth of talent pool
- Attractive benefit programs

Some examples of past performance themes are:

- Overall corporate experience
- Years in business
- Total number of contracts performed
- Total number of relevant contracts
- Total number person years relevant experience
- Performance record
- The customer's need is our core business (only if true!)
- Experience with this client
- Quotes from customers
- Reliability
- Number/types of deliverables
- Lessons learned
- Transition experience
- Reduced learning curve
- Positive Contractor Performance Assessment Rating System (CPAR) ratings
- Initiatives and innovations
- Breadth of experience

Key Personnel. Key personnel are often one of the top evaluation criteria in a services RFP. They are even more important on bids that require oral presentations. I have had the experience of winning competitive bids at orals after having been number two or three in the technical evaluation. This is critical if you're a small company going up against larger companies with the ability and resources to write outstanding proposals. In other words, a few solid key personnel who are liked by the client can seize the day.

The ideal key personnel are known, trusted, and respected by the customer. This means you have introduced them prior to the RFP being released. Or, they are already known from prior work you have performed at this agency. Or, you have hired them from an incumbent contractor or on a contingent basis.

I have seen companies win bids with key personnel who had relatively weak resumes but were really liked by the client. Which, of course, speaks to the importance of establishing strong relationships with the customer during the capture phase of the competition.

Because of their skills and seniority, key personnel often have salaries at the higher end of their pay range. The staffing mix or balance you bid is a critical decision on lowest cost technically acceptable bids as opposed to best value or best technical and management acquisitions.

No matter how desired or qualified your key personnel are, they must be willing to be bid in the proposal and available upon award. In the '80s and '90s, some services contractors got a well-deserved reputation for the unethical practice of bait and switching. They bid John knowing that he would not be available and so delivered Mary upon award. Fortunately, I've seen less of this in the past decade. Still, there are occasions where the time between proposal submittal and government evaluation and award is so protracted that some of the people you bid are no longer available. In this case, anything goes!

Proposal pricing. Understanding the funding status of a federal opportunity (see the following Figure) is one of the most ignored but critical bid

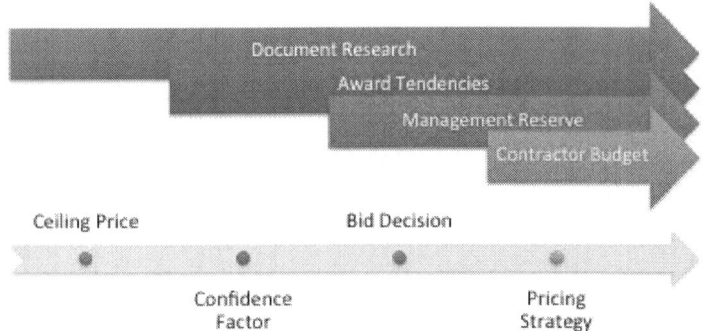

factors. Identifying the funding source and whether the project is in the budget and stable is key to determining if the program is viable. This analysis will help determine the probable ceiling price, a funding estimate confidence factor, the financial rationale for making a bid decision and serve as a critical element of the pricing strategy. The should-cost process is highly dependent on the dynamics of the pursuit and, of course, availability of information.

On the other hand, it would be a mistake to think that you will win the contract just because your price came in below the government's cost estimate. In the current annoying LPTA bidding environment, the 'should cost' is like high tide in the island harbor where I live. Boats safely docked at high tide, like competitive bids that are too high, face the danger of being stranded when the water flows out. A sure recipe for competitive pricing regret.

You need to have competitive pricing information readily available to develop winning pricing strategies. Five key components for determining what price you should bid are:

1. **Available funding.** Determine ceiling price and confidence factor for the target pursuit; informs your bid/no bid decision and bid strategy development.
2. **Should cost.** Analyze what the government believes the pursuit should cost based on past performance and future influencing factors. Provides you with a critical data point to make bid decisions and develop pricing strategy.
3. **Price competitiveness.** Analyze your cost pool structure and cost elements, bidding practices related to these pools, and disclosure statement details to determine if you're competitive in a particular market.
4. **Financial analysis.** Perform reverse engineering on contracts with available financial information to determine burdened labor rates, direct labor rates, average rate per hour and total contract value, as appropriate. Provides you with data to assist in determining whether to bid on a recompete or similar contract and if so, what the competition, including the incumbent(s), might bid. Also, what are the agency's past award statistics (mostly low price, best-value, or mostly incumbents win).
5. **Wrap Rate analysis.** Research GSA and other rate schedule, labor category, burdened labor rates for your specific service areas and target agencies; map these labor categories to various salary surveys; and calculate the burden to each labor category. Identify and discard gamed rates and average remaining rates into competitive wrap rates. This analysis provides you with insight into the wrap rates of competitors and bidding strategies.

We've all probably experienced the feeling of regret between the action should have taken instead of the action we took. This feeling of regret or second-guessing is summed up in the expression *woulda coulda shoulda.*

Proposal reviews. One of the most important but often overlooked aspects of successful proposal development is the institution of a thorough review process. Depending on the proposal timeframe, this may involve two or three reviews. The size and complexity of the proposal usually dictates the number of reviewers required. There should also be a review chair.

The purpose of the initial proposal review, sometimes called a pink team, is to focus on the strategy, cost approach, visuals, and organization of the proposal. The proposal manager usually begins by presenting the proposal requirements, strategy, and storyboard or, if completed, draft proposal materials. The pink team reviews the sections assigned by the review chair and critiques the use of themes and discriminators, the effectiveness of the visuals (graphics and tables), the presentation of the offer and the cohesiveness of the overall proposal. This first review is a very important part the process. It allows the evaluators and senior management to see exactly what the proposal team has in mind. If the writers have deviated from the original proposal strategy it can be easily corrected without losing a significant amount of time.

The second proposal review, or red team review, should perform a "pretend" customer technical evaluation of the proposal. The red team members must have a clear understanding of the requirements as outlined in the RFP. They must be conscious of all issues addressed in the pink team and kickoff meetings. They must review the proposal for full compliance in addition to strategy, cost approach, visuals, and organization.

The red team should critique all aspects of the proposal including themes and discriminators, effectiveness of the visuals (graphics and tables), presentation of the offer and, finally, the cohesiveness of the overall proposal. *To avoid new direction late in the proposal process, red team members should also have participated in the earlier proposal kick-off meeting and pink team review.*

In many instances, this is the last review of the proposal before delivery; therefore, this review is critical to the process. The feedback that is provided at this stage in the process is more important now than at any other time. It is imperative at this juncture that the red team provides clear, detailed direction to the proposal team and not cursory or high-level comments. If there are serious problems with specific sections of the proposal, it's not uncommon for a red team member to re-write them in their entirety. Due to time constraints, this should be avoided.

If time permits, a third and final smaller gold team review should be conducted. The number of participants may vary but no one new should be added to the mix. This review team (individual) should concentrate primarily on last minute proposal compliance and quality as opposed to content.

Obviously, proposal development (see Shipley) is a much more in-depth discipline. A proposal development guide I prepared for one large integrator was almost 200 pages long!

Five considerations to start the new year

I wrote this piece at the start of 2020. – Mark

I will ignore the elephant in the room and not discuss the ever-present beginning of yet another fiscal year continuing resolution. As I re-read John Keegan's *Intelligence in War*, I keep thinking about what kinds of intelligence companies need to survive, then thrive, in GovCon.

Let's start with the basics:

Contract intelligence. As we all know, SAM, FPDS, FBO, and more will be merged into one system under GSA. I don't hold out any great hope for ease-of-use in the near term, but I hope I'm wrong. When and if it comes together, it should be a great platform.

In the meantime, you need to have current, actionable information. I use Bloomberg Government and I'm quite pleased with it, especially as they add features based on customer input. GovWin, FedMine and others are also available. If you use Deltek's software, GovWin dovetails nicely. Regardless, you need the contract data to map out where you're going.

I also have numerous news feeds from GovCon trade media, blogs, and podcasts that I monitor.

Live networking. Live networking events such as the Washington Technology Power Breakfasts are an excellent place to find people interested in the same issues as you.

Associations such as AFCEA, ACT/IAC, and PSC are equally important as you get further into the year and beyond market planning. The exposure you can receive by actively participating in events and associations is essential to your company's growth.

In an earlier chapter, I explained that the same criteria I used for picking events and networking venues applies to the associations that you might want to join. The pedigree of the organization, a.k.a. its background, the networking opportunities, and the education offered by the association are the key factors when making your choice.

While I only listed three associations above, there are a variety of very specialized groups throughout the GovCon ecosystem. Some of these focus on specific agencies, such as the NASA Contractors Group which meets in Greenbelt, Maryland, or a CEO group I won't name that focuses on doing business at Fort Meade. There are others, such as the Government Blockchain Association, that concentrate on specific technologies. Finding these groups is not always easy but can be critical to your survival and growth.

Two other factors that I've already discussed in earlier chapters are account/agency-based marketing and leveraging an experienced outside POV.

Consultant support. One other factor is to consider is bringing in a consultant with deep market knowledge to help you review your go to market plan before you start implementing it. Host a brainstorming session with your leadership team and invite this expert to review your plans beforehand, then come in and give various "what if" scenarios.

Over the years both Mike and I have participated in a number of these as the outside expert on marketing issues which overlap with sales, business development, and capture issues. Often, I've identified gaps in leveraging associations, social media and traditional media, and events that have helped companies establish deeper connections with current agencies or to go after new business. Sometimes those inside the company are too close to the issue to see some of these gaps.

I started this chapter by referencing John Keegan's *Intelligence in War*. Sun Tzu's *The Art of War* also references leveraging intelligence to gain a significant advantage.

My final tip on things to consider when you're proceeding with new year and beyond planning is to *gather intelligence* from multiple sources that can be used by your executive team and frontline managers. Have an internal venue for sharing that intelligence and having it analyzed by stakeholders in marketing, sales, BD, capture, proposals, engineering/technology, recruiting, and finance. Regularly sharing these insights with the executive team will ensure course corrections are made in a timely manner.

Know all your contract requirements

I have had this discussion with every manager I've coached and included it in every presentation since 2000. – Mike

It is surprising how many proposal managers or project managers are unaware of all their projects' requirements. Not knowing your overall contract or specific task order requirements is like trying to hike somewhere without a map and then being shocked when you don't reach your destination.

- Understanding the requirements is one of the best risk mitigation strategies a PM can employ. Obtain and review a copy of the technical and pricing proposal from your company contracts department.
- Pay particular attention to any gaps between what was proposed, the final contract and your plan. It's not unusual, especially on larger procurements, for there to have been a long time between proposal submittal and contract award. Company salaries and overhead costs may have changed and new circumstances such as product releases and resource availability may impact your ability to deliver to the proposed schedule. All these factors will need to be taken into consideration and, where necessary, coordinated with the client upon contract award.
- Study each of the "shall" statements in the RFP as well as in your company's proposal including specific deliverables. These requirements may be documented in the proposal traceability compliance matrix.
- Look to see if there are any ancillary requirements such as special equipment, security clearances, technology specialists, certifications, or unique training.

- Make sure you understand how and when you will be reporting to the customer.
- Compare the commitments and assumptions you made in the proposal with your understanding of the RFP and Statement of Work requirements. Make a list of any ambiguities and anything you aren't sure you can complete. Obtain clarification of these items from your contracts department or the client.
- Alert the security, facilities, and information technology department of any special requirements.

Remember, that a failure to manage to the contract requirements baseline almost always results in significant problems including contractor failure to deliver and customer requirements scope creep.

Three fiscal year end tactics

Several marketing strategies I've written about are now, with the pandemic, more important than ever. – Mark

The Covid 19 crisis has forced Feds and contractors alike to a new level of "digital transformation," a forced migration to tools we were aware of but not necessarily using often or well: online meetings, telework, and social networks like LinkedIn, Twitter, and Facebook.

With the physical re-opening of federal sites still in question, the need to adapt has never been greater. I've heard from different sources that federal offices will not return to any semblance of normal this year. In the meantime, here are a few ideas to win more business at the end of fiscal.

First, relevant content, well written or produced, then properly deployed after production. Content can take many forms such as articles, blog posts, videos, podcasts, webinars, and white papers. Studies from Market Connections, Inc, Hinge Marketing, and others have not only demonstrated the value of content in the procurement process but have shown it to be a critical factor when you're targeting specific contracts, going after business with a specific agency, or developing and showcasing an area of expertise. Producing the content is step one, putting it where your target audience will find it's step two.

All content should be resident on your web site under a "Resources" button. After that, share it via social media and email. If you post it on LinkedIn, it automatically goes to your 1st degree connections via their "Home" page. If someone else shares it, it goes into their 1st degree network the same way. Your content should be educational in nature and avoid any overt sales message. Just include contact info at the end and encourage readers and viewers to share.

Second, virtual events. By now, we should all be ZOOM-masters, right? I was on ZOOM before Covid 19 sequestered us, but now I feel like I can't live without it. ZOOM is massively more personal than a call.

Many events, even larger ones, have gone virtual with varying degrees of success. For those that didn't quite succeed, the problem was often with technical infrastructure or the partner who produced the event. Vetting your virtual event provider and testing capacity is key; so, start by asking your peers who they are using. If you attend an event that works, or that doesn't work well, find out which platform was used.

If you're hosting an event for govies, make certain it's on a platform approved by their agency. If it's FedRAMP compliant, you should be OK. If not, rethink your platform. Clearly, virtual events are here to stay.

Third, social selling. Social selling has been growing in importance over the last few years but now is critical. LinkedIn is the primary venue for this and the traffic on LinkedIn since the "stay at home" order has risen significantly.

Social selling is not traditional selling. It's the art and science of getting on the radar of a defined audience and staying on the radar in a non-intrusive way by leveraging social networks. It's not designed to replace traditional sales or business development, but to supplement and support them.

Sharing your content is a social selling technique. Finding, liking, and commenting on content shared by your prospects, is another technique. "Following" your prospects before reaching out is yet another.

Reaching out to connect with your prospective audience can be a social selling technique if you don't send the LinkedIn connection "form letter." Find a way to put the connection request *in context of what the prospect does and what you bring to the table*, but not a sales context.

Each of these tactics works regardless of the Covid 19 crisis, but they are more important now that we don't currently have the face-to-face option of our normal end-of-fiscal year. If you have any questions about any of these, please reach out to me via LinkedIn. Best of fortunes for your federal "busy season"!

Manage client expectations to win more business

Several years ago, I met with 25 industry project managers in an open forum to discuss how we could improve project implementation. – Mike

Here are some hard-earned client satisfaction lessons learned as well as ways to set, monitor and manage client expectations to increase effectiveness and secure more follow-on business.

- **Identify your stakeholders.** Who has a vested interest in your project? Who has the resources you need or who will ultimately approve your project? Make sure you build good rapport with these people.
- **Define success criteria.** You and your client should agree on what constitutes project completion. If you don't achieve this understanding, you may never finish the project. Success criteria are especially important on fixed-price deliverable tasks.
- **Get a solid start.** Conduct thorough kickoff meetings and carefully document objectives, milestones, and client responsibilities.
- **Review project status.** Develop and maintain a project plan. Review this plan with your team and with your client on a weekly or biweekly basis.
- **Know your contract.** Refer to your contract before agreeing to additional tasks. You're responsible for controlling the scope of work as well as any changes made to it.
- **Be careful what you promise.** Be willing to say no when something that your client wants is not in the baseline requirements or SOW or when a request is unreasonable

or unethical. Furthermore, as the expert, you should say no when it is something that would not be in the client's best interest. In such a case, you can say something like, "Our experience tells us that..." Remember, that when you must say no, try to offer a more attractive alternative that solves the client's problem to show that you're looking out for their best interest.

- **Actively seek feedback.** Listen to your team members and client regarding what is and what isn't going well. You cannot fix a problem that you don't know about or want to know about. Issues that you ignore or refuse to hear could surface later to torpedo your project.
- **Avoid surprises.** Develop contingency plans when you discover potential problems with the project, such as risks and limitations that may affect the outcome.
- **Communicate regularly.** Recognize the warning signs that your client relationship is in danger. These include a lack of regular communication between you and your client; fear of talking to your client about something specific or, even worse, about anything at all; and uncertainty about your client's approval of what you're going to deliver.
- Be proactive. Get your project out of trouble by listening to your client and understanding specific concerns. You may want to bring along an executive when you need to demonstrate commitment or when you have bad news. Finally, be honest –

It's easier to remember the truth you told a month ago than the lie you told yesterday!

Short attention spans are a challenge

I'm fascinated with the impact of technology on an already too high GovCon attention deficit. – Mark

From 1989 to 1995, HBO presciently produced a comedy that predicted a phenomenon beyond our control, the ever-decreasing attention span. The show, *Short Attention Span Theatre*, soon become known as SAST (representing yet another growing phenomenon -- the *acronymization* of our language…talk about a short attention span).

As one might surmise from the name, SAST was a series of short skits and interviews, many of which were LOL (sic) hilarious. Among the hosts was a rising comedic star, Jon Stewart. This was eminently watchable TV for the simple reason that things happened quickly, and if you only had a few minutes to spare, you could watch, laugh, and move on without fear of missing a plot twist. Look it up on YouTube -- it stands the test of time

I did a little research on attention spans recently and found that some people's attention spans (including my co-author's) were now under ten seconds. That's right, ***TEN seconds.***

I won't speculate as to why our attention spans are getting shorter, except to say that with the various technologies available, the craving for instant gratification continues to outdistance our desire for deeper understanding. I'd blame Gordon Moore (see below), but he was simply pointing out the obvious.

Not only are attention spans getting shorter, but most people are multi-tasking, especially the younger ones, which further reduces the attention given to each task. So, now we get to the crux of the matter: in marketing "content is king." Companies seeking to grow market share have an ever-increasing need to put content into the hands of people who make buying decisions. Unfortunately, it's likely that their audience lacks the time to consume the tons of daily content that's coming at them from multiple directions. And, like most, they probably have a shrinking attention span.

We have is the collision of short attention spans with the desire to *get* the attention of decision makers, an audience that may or may not pay attention to your content even if it crosses their screen or even lands in their inbox.

Add to this the fact that content is being produced and shared at a breakneck pace. Think of this as *Moore's Law (1)* where computing speed is replaced by the amount of content being generated, and instead of doubling every two years (Moore's original concept), now it takes maybe a couple of months to double the amount of content being generated. As Moore implied, this is not a reversible condition.

With this addition to our "content is king" premise, *how do we get the attention of the audience we seek?*

Many marketers understand that *being concise is key*. I call it the *word-per-idea ratio (2)* where you strive to keep the ratio as tight as possible while retaining the ability to convey a concept. This is the reason so many business videos, podcasts, and blog posts are short. It's why I try to keep most of my articles and blog posts to under 500 words. Make one good point and make it fast. Next time you have something to share, people are likely to remember that you make your point quickly, and they may be more likely to give you another look. Violate that by boring them with verbosity or rehashed ideas and you're toast.

Of course, the biggest challenge is getting your content in the queue of the decision makers. Then even if it gets in the queue, a variation of *Heisenberg's uncertainty principle* (3) occurs: *the timing* -- will it be found and read or will it miss being seen because it was not delivered in the venue (LinkedIn, Facebook, Twitter, etc.) when your prospect was present?

Short attention spans + too much content + timing issues = black hole absorbing unseen content.

There is no simple solution to this puzzle. However, there are ways to increase the odds in your favor, including:

- Try to produce good content that is germane to your audience.
- Feature only one main idea per piece of content.
- Use a compelling headline or title that highlights the topic you will discuss.
- In written pieces, use graphics.
- Cite original sources as necessary and link to those original sources.
- Hashtag people and companies mentioned.
- Re-purpose the content into multiple formats.
- Place the content in venues where it will most likely find the right audience.
- Place it in those venues *more than once* (retweeting is great, posting on LinkedIn *in different places* should work).

- Send it directly to those you really need to reach IF you have a relationship with them.
- Generate content on a regular basis, not on rare occasion.
- Make certain the content is edited for clarity and grammar.
- Ask viewers and readers to share ("If you liked this, please share it with those who might find it useful.").
- Care and feed your regular viewers/commenters – respond to comments and remember to say thank you.
- All your content (or links to it) should be in one location on your web site.

Is this too much to keep in mind when producing content? Initially, yes, but most of it becomes muscle memory with practice.

If I come up with a more practical solution, I'll (humbly) call it *Amtower's Content Marketing Law. AND, if you like this chapter, please share this book with your network!*

Notes:

(1) Moore's law: IT executive Gordon Moore wrote in 1965 that the speed of computing would double every two years predicated on the number of transistors a microchip can hold.

(2) I first heard the phrase "word per idea ratio" from Chris Trelease, then with telemarketing firm Sturner and Klein. I worked there while in graduate school and a short time beyond that, and I met and worked with some great people.

(3) Uncertainty principle, also called Heisenberg uncertainty principle or indeterminacy principle, statement, articulated (1927) by the German physicist Werner Heisenberg, that the position and the velocity of an object cannot both be measured exactly, at the same time, even in theory.

Start re-compete preparation early

Several few decades of watching incumbents lose recompetes because they weren't prepared led me to document some best practices. – Mike

A too often ignored but major business development activity every PM needs to be aware of is to perform early re-compete capture activities. Of course, as discussed in an earlier chapter, maintaining customer satisfaction is a major element of winning a re-compete. But, waiting until the last minute to prepare and execute a capture plan is a recipe for disaster.

At least several months before your contract is to be re-competed, you should define and implement the winning capture strategy. Be an internal champion for necessary capture and proposal resources. Understand the client's needs and biases. For instance, is someone in the client's organization or a small business contractor pushing to have your work set-aside for small or small disadvantaged business competition? And, if so, can you or your organization's representative make a convincing argument why this acquisition change would jeopardize contract performance? As the PM, it's your responsibility to keep the organization focused on the capture of your re-compete.

Every re-compete should have some level of capture plan. This plan should include:

- Acquisition strategy
- Competitive analysis
- Project improvement actions

- Positioning
- Customer requirements changes
- Design to cost
- Teaming/subcontract changes
- Pricing strategy including determining the most likely Price-to-Win range

In general, the re-compete process involves understanding the client's acquisition strategy, the potential competition including who's teaming together and their strengths and weaknesses. Also, as the incumbent, how you can correct any of your weaknesses prior to the acquisition process start. Depending on the size and complexity of a project, the capture manager for your re-compete might be you as the current PM, an assigned capture manager or an organization executive.

Re-competes should follow your organization's BD and bid decision process and utilize the sales lead tracking system.

The first consideration is to determine whether your organization wants to continue to perform this work. Factors to consider include:

- Has it been profitable?
- Is the work doable? Is the customer too difficult to work with?
- Does the client want you to win again (are they satisfied with your support)?
- Does it take too much management attention to oversee the project for the realized revenue and profit?
- If a very small task, does it have sufficient expansion potential to justify bidding again or would you better off

subcontracting or handing off the work to a small business partner?

Assuming the answer is yes, some key capture positioning questions you should consider are:

- Is it time to replace any key staff (does the client like them)?
- Do you still have the right subcontractors?
- Are there any weaknesses that need to be corrected?
- Can you make these changes prior to the proposal period?
- What are the key themes and discriminators?

Too often, PMs assume that because the client is satisfied with your performance, that they'll give your organization high proposal scores. However, this assumes your key clients are on the proposal evaluation team. This isn't always the case.

Make sure you describe the features and benefits of your technical approach even if the client knows this already. Give them the information they need to be able to score you highly in the proposal evaluation.

Describe your management approach including staffing, your organizational structure and task management process. Include a management risk assessment and mitigation discussion to demonstrate your understanding of the job. This is a proposal technique that can really discriminate an incumbent from the competition.

Regarding pricing, consider whether you need to be more aggressive in the pricing of the offer. There will most likely be one or more other companies bidding an aggressively low price hoping to unseat you as the incumbent. Sometimes this means you'll need to replace some personnel and hire more junior staff (except for key personnel the client loves). Don't just assume the client will pay a premium to keep you around. Also, do you know what this $ delta is? In other words, avoid drinking your own bath water! In today's lowest-priced-technically-acceptable bidding environment, complacent contractors rarely win follow-on business.

Six tips for surviving as a consultant

Consulting isn't for the faint-of-heart. However, here are some tips for those wishing to be independent services provider. – Mark

Over the years several people have come up to me at various events and said something like, "I can do what you do." Usually I simply respond, "Go for it." If they do go for it, and they are good at what they do, I may advise them on how to set up a consulting business, properly price their services and advertise themselves. I even started a formal six-month program for this purpose.

However, most will not survive as a solo consultant. You need to be a big *self-motivator*, be able to work *by yourself*, endure dry (no $) spells, know what business to turn down and what to accept, know how to *position yourself* in the market and more.

And you need to define this expertise in a way that resonates with the market niche that may require your help. Many of those in transition find themselves in the role of consultant, often in a default mode and often what they hope will be a temporary situation. Regardless, if you find yourself bearing the title "consultant," here are five tips to get you going.

First and foremost, know your strengths and your limitations, and be painfully honest with yourself as you write these down. Please notice I said, *"write these down."* Writing down your strengths and weaknesses reinforces them in your mind. You aren't going to share them with anyone so being honest with yourself should be easier. And remember, weaknesses need not be permanent.

Are your strengths something someone or some company will pay an outside consultant for? You're looking to pinpoint a specific area of expertise where you excel. You need to define this expertise in a way that resonates with the market niche that may require your help.

Second, *define* the niche that needs what you do. You may offer a service that smaller contractors require as they don't currently have the infrastructure or pipeline to support having that skill internally.

Your service may appeal to specific job function areas (business development, audits, marketing, back office, contract management, factoring, specialized insurance, and the like). In all likelihood you can start to define your niche in terms of company size and functional area. If you can differentiate further, perhaps a regional/geographic focus, do so.

Third, establish your *credentials*. You will need a web site and a strong LinkedIn profile. Both should share how you developed this area of expertise and highlight anything that makes you special.

A big part of establishing credentials is *content*. Your content should be designed to showcase your *expertise*, an educated point of view about your niche. It can include commentary on current market events, regulations shaping your niche, useful marketing tactics, and more.

Fourth, know *who to pitch* to in an organization. The smaller the company, the higher up you should pitch. In the late 1980s, I was sharing with business friend a problem I was having. This one marketing guy would attend my seminars but never ask me to come over to his company headquarters to discuss what they were doing. My friend laughed at me and said, "You should be talking directly to the CEO, not the marketing guy." Within a few weeks I had a lunch meeting with Dendy Young, CEO of Falcon Microsystems, and we've been good friends ever since.

Fifth, if you're in the consulting biz to stay, *be prepared to morph*. When I first started my company, I became an expert in direct marketing to the government via snail mail. I've adapted and morphed several times in the past 35 years, through the launch of the web, the initial confusion over email marketing, the evolution of web 2.0, and finally the creation and deployment of social networks. At each step along the way I've had to adapt and adopt. *Push your boundaries, but not on someone else's dime.* Becoming a consultant isn't as simple as adding a line to your LinkedIn profile, though some think so.

Sixth, only accept assignments when you can *add value*. If you're asked to do something that isn't an area of strength, pass. Instead, recommend someone you know, trust, and who's quite good at what the customer needs. Doing so will bolster your value in return.

Afterword: Why we wrote this book

This book was born out of a few Zoom discussions we had with each other in late 2021. We waxed philosophically about the complexity of selling to the government and the absence of written concrete lessons learned that can be found in one location. It seemed to us that too many of our fellow professionals kept making the same mistakes.

We've both worked hard for many decades to add value to the Federal government contracting market. We've each seen things, talked to hundreds of people, and advised hundreds of companies. In the process, we gathered ideas -- some old, some new -- that we believed needed to see the light of day. This resulted in literally hundreds of articles, some of which we consider timeless and so worthy of being included in this book.

We enjoy writing for a variety of reasons; certainly, to share with others, but also to gain insight into our own thinking. Each of us continues to share ideas on multiple forums, but we find tremendous satisfaction in the written word and a well-turned phrase, especially when an important idea comes to life.

Finally, we LOVE getting feedback. So please leave a review on Amazon or share it with us through email or on LinkedIn.

markamtower@gmail.com
www.linkedin.com/in/markamtower
mikelisagor@celerityworks.com
www.linkedin.com/in/mikelisagor

And thank you for reading this. We wish you continued success in the coming years!

Made in the USA
Middletown, DE
09 February 2022